Programming the M68000

Tim King and Brian Knight

ADDISON-WESLEY PUBLISHING COMPANY
Reading, Massachusetts   Menlo Park, California
London   Amsterdam   Don Mills, Ontario   Sydney

This book is in the
Addison-Wesley Microcomputer Books
Popular Series

Set by the authors in Helvesan and Messenger using a pagination program written by T. J. King and running on a 68000.

Cover illustration by Stuart Hughes.

Printed in Finland by OTAVA. Member of Finnprint.

ISBN 0-201-11730-4
ABCDEFGHIJ-876543

Contents

Preface

We have organised this book so that it can be read from beginning
to end; read in this way it presents a complete introduction to
assembly language programming for the 68000. For the more
experienced reader, a summary of the instruction set is provided as
an appendix. This gives brief details of each instruction and a page
reference to a more complete description in the main text.

The information about the successors to the 68000, the 68010 and
the 68020, has been obtained from advance publicity from Motorola.
We would like to thank Motorola for this information, and also for
permission to include material from their documentation on the 68000
itself. Motorola wish us to include the following disclaimer.

Motorola assumes no responsibility for any inaccuracies in this text,
and reserves the right to make changes to any of the products
described to improve reliability, function or design. Motorola does not
assume any liability arising out of the application or use of any
product described herein. No licence is conveyed under patent rights
in any form. Specifications of new products are subject to change
without notice.

We would like to thank various colleagues at the Universities of
Cambridge and Bath for their help with this book, and particularly
Dr. Arthur Norman for permission to include his long division routine.
We would also like to thank Agi Lehar-Graham for drawing the
diagrams and Jessica King for her help with the index.

March 1983   Tim King
                                                          Brian Knight

Chapter 1

Introduction

As its title implies, this book concentrates on the 68000 microprocessor as seen by the programmer, and almost completely avoids discussion of hardware issues. It is aimed at the reader who has access to a built 68000 system, and is concerned with how to program it effectively.

The book is self-contained, introducing the architecture of the machine and its instruction set in a logical order. It can be read without any need to refer to Motorola documentation for the 68000, although the latter should be consulted for details such as the bit pattern of each instruction.

The discussion of each instruction points out any unusual features of its operation, both pitfalls to avoid and particular uses. Many of these features are of the kind which are easily overlooked when reading the formal definition, and which will waste time and cause confusion when they are tripped over in practice. As each instruction is introduced, one or more worked examples are given to illustrate its use. These examples are intended to be useful code fragments which can be employed in larger programs. They are used here to build up a small monitor program which provides simple input/output and debugging facilities.

The remainder of this chapter gives a brief history of the evolution of microprocessors, and compares the 68000 with others in current use. It then gives a general description of the features of the 68000 and some typical applications. The second chapter introduces the assembler syntax employed in later chapters, and explains the operand addressing modes of the instructions.

The following chapters present the instructions in related groups. Chapter three describes the various ways in which data items can be moved about and compared with one another. The concepts of stacks and subroutines are introduced in chapter four. Chapter five covers the instructions provided for doing arithmetic and includes routines for multiplication and division of larger numbers than can be handled directly. The logical operations for working on individual bits are described in chapter six, and they are used in the code of a store allocation package. Chapter seven deals with interrupts and traps, illustrating the writing of interrupt routines, and the use of traps as

1

system calls, for error detection, and for debugging programs. The final chapter gives a complete example of a small monitor, which handles terminal input and output and provides a convenient environment for debugging other programs.

Evolution of microprocessors

A constant trend throughout the 40-odd year history of electronic computers is that as time goes on it becomes possible to make them smaller and smaller. The earliest machines used thermionic valves, required a large room to house them, and consumed huge amounts of power. The invention of transistors enabled the size and power consumption to be reduced by several times. In the 1960s, it became possible to produce integrated circuits consisting of a few transistors and associated components fabricated in one small chip of silicon, making it possible to build a computer in one cabinet of reasonable size. In the early 1970s the technology of integrated circuits had advanced to the point where it was possible to put all of the central processor of a simple computer onto one chip – the first microprocessors. Since then we have seen a decade of rapid progress, and there are now available microprocessors which have not compromised in power in order to fit on one chip, and which compete directly with computers produced from discrete components.

The earliest microprocessors which found appreciable use were those which could operate on only 4 bits of data at a time, such as the Intel 4040. These were suitable for simple control applications (e.g. vending machines, alarm systems) and unsophisticated arcade games but little more, as they were slow, cumbersome for data in useful units, and could address only a very limited amount of memory.

It was after the introduction of 8-bit machines that microprocessors became widespread. The most popular of these include the Intel 8080 and 8085, the Zilog Z80 (which has the 8080 instructions as a subset of its instruction set), the MOS Technology 6502, and the Motorola 6800 and 6809. It is usual for machines described as 'N-bit processors' to have some capability for handling items 2N bits in size. Most of the above can perform arithmetical and logical operations on 16-bit quantities, though the 6502 has no 16-bit internal registers.

Some of these 8-bit chips became very cheap, so were viable for building into other equipment, and could also be used for moderately powerful and inexpensive home computers. At the time of writing, almost all personal computers intended for domestic or small business use are based on either the Z80 or the 6502.

As 8-bit micros evolved, there was a tendency towards removing 'untidy' features of their implementation, such as requiring several power supply voltages, multi-phase clock inputs, or multiplexed address/data lines. It is now normal for new designs to need a single 5 volt supply, a single phase clock input (or just a crystal to control an internal clock), and to have each connecting pin performing just one function. Some (such as the Z80) provide assistance with refreshing dynamic semiconductor memory.

Another development has been the introduction of limited single-chip computers, such as the TMS9940. These have some memory holding a fixed program (ROM) and some alterable memory

(RAM) as well as the processor, enabling special purpose computers to be produced in a single package, improving the ease with which they can be wired up to other circuitry. Such devices are most suited to being designed for, and built into, a particular piece of equipment.

From the software point of view, the next important development was the introduction of 16-bit and 32-bit microprocessors at the end of the 1970s. These blurred the distinction between mini-computers and micro-computers, as most of the common minis were 16-bit machines. Among the first such chips were the Texas TMS9900 series, Intel 8086, TMS99000, Zilog Z8000, and the subject of this book, the Motorola 68000. Newcomers which are not widely available at the time of writing include the National Semiconductor NS16032 and Intel's 80286 and iAPX 432.

The 68000 stands out from its predecessors as being perhaps the first microprocessor with an architecture and instruction set resembling that of a large mainframe. It has a very large directly accessible address space, the ability to manipulate items 8, 16, and 32 bits in size, 16 registers each 32 bits long, some instructions intended to ease the compilation of high-level languages, a supervisor mode which can be used to prevent unprivileged programs accessing certain regions of memory or directly initiating I/O operations, and provision for multi-processor interlocks.

The following tables present a brief specification of each of the above processors for comparison. Note that some care should be exercised when comparing the speeds of different processors, as later models of a particular machine are usually capable of running at greater clock rates than earlier ones. Thus speed can reflect how long a machine has been on the market, rather than indicating the potential of the design.

MOS Technology 6502

Direct Address Range:	64 Kbytes
Quickest Instruction:	0.5 microseconds (4MHz clock)
General Registers:	1 (8 bit)
Other Registers:	2 8-bit index registers, 8-bit stack pointer
Interrupt levels:	2

Bytes in the lowest page of memory can be paired for use in 16-bit indexing. The instruction set offers a good selection of addressing modes, but there are no instructions for directly manipulating data items longer than 8 bits.

Zilog Z80

Direct Address Range: 64 Kbytes
Quickest Instruction: 1 microsecond (4MHz clock)
General Registers: 7 (8-bit) + duplicate set
Other Registers: 2 16-bit index registers, 16-bit stack pointer
Interrupt levels: 2

The 8-bit registers can be paired and used as 3 16-bit registers. The instruction set supports 16-bit arithmetic and block moves and searches in memory. The instructions of the Intel 8080/8085 are. a subset of the Z80 instructions.

Motorola 6809

Direct Address Range: 64 Kbytes
Quickest Instruction: 2 microseconds (2MHz clock)
General Registers: 2 (8 bit)
Other Registers: 2 index registers, 2 stack pointers (16-bit)
Interrupt levels: 3

The two 8-bit accumulators can be combined as a 16-bit register. The instruction set allows limited 16-bit arithmetic and 8 * 8 bit multiplication.

Intel 8086

Direct Address Range: 1 Mbyte
Quickest Instruction: 0.4 microseconds (5MHz clock)
General Registers: 4 (16 bit)
Other Registers: base registers, stack/index
Interrupt levels: 2

The address space is divided into 4 segments (code, data, stack, and extra) which may overlap. All addressing is relative to segment base registers; a segment base address is a multiple of 16. The 8086 has 24 operand addressing modes, can do signed and unsigned 16-bit multiplication and division, has loop instructions, and can do an indivisible read-modify-write memory access. The Intel 8088 processor can run all the same software as the 8086, but has an 8-oit (rather than 16-bit) external bus, and so can be used with 8-bit support chips.

TMS9900 series

Direct Address Range: 64 Kbytes (TMS9900)
Quickest Instruction: 2 microseconds (4MHz clock)
General Registers: 16 (but held in RAM, not internally)
Other Registers: Workspace pointer (i.e. registers)
Interrupt Levels: 16 (TMS9900,9995), 4 (others)

The registers are held in an area of RAM pointed to by the workspace pointer register. In the TMS9995 they are cached internally. There are instructions for 16-bit multiply and divide.

This is a family of processors with a common instruction set:

9900   basic model
9940   single chip computer with built-in RAM and ROM
9980/81 8-bit bus only, can address only 16 Kbytes
9985   single chip computer with built-in RAM (but no ROM)
9995   registers cached internally

TMS99000

Direct Address Range: 64 Kbytes
Quickest Instruction: 0.5' microseconds (6 MHz clock)
General Registers: 16 (held in RAM)
Other Registers: workspace pointer (pointer to registers)
Interrupt Levels: 16

The 99000 can address up to 16M bytes of segmented memory using a support chip. It can add, subtract, and shift 32-bit quantities. It has a supervisor mode, and test-and-set instruction for synchronizing multiple processors. Instruction decoding is such that instruction codes which are not built-in can be handled by user microcode (held on chip), user code in external RAM, or by an attached processor.

Zilog Z8000

Direct Address Range: 8 Mbytes
Quickest Instruction: 0.75 microseconds (8MHz clock)
General Registers: 16 (16 bits)
Other Registers: memory refresh counter, status area pointer
Interrupt Levels: 2

There are six address spaces, each of which can be 8 Mbytes in size. There are two versions of the chip: a 'segmented' one with 8 Mbytes address range, and an 'unsegmented' one with 64 Kbytes address range. The first 8 registers can be used as 16 8-bit registers. The registers can be used as 16 * 16 bits, 8 * 32 bits, or 4 * 64 bits. Multiply is available for 16-bit or 32-bit operands, divide for 32-bit or 64-bit dividends. Shifting can be performed on 8, 16, or 32-bit registers. There is a supervisor mode, test-and-set instruction, and other instructions for interfacing multiple processors. The Z8000 has instructions for block copy, and character translation. It has 8 address modes, but only 4 types of processor trap.

Motorola 68000

Direct Address Range: 16 Mbytes
Quickest Instruction: 0.5 microseconds (8 MHz clock)
General Registers: 16 (32 bits)
Other Registers: user stack register
Interrupt Levels: 7

The internal architecture is 32 bits wide, and most operations can be performed on 8, 16, or 32-bit values. The only important omission from a full 32-bit capability is the lack of 32-bit multiply and divide. The address space is linear. The registers are divided into 8 data registers and 8 address registers; some operations can use only one type. One of the address registers is duplicated; which one is available depends on whether the processor is in supervisor or user state. There are 14 operand addressing modes, many types of processor trap, and instructions available only in supervisor state. A 'Test and Set' instruction is provided for read-modify-write memory access.

National Semiconductor NS16032 (from preliminary specification)

Direct Address Range: 16 Mbytes
General registers: 8 (32 bits)
Other Registers: stack frame pointer, static variables pointer, user/interrupt stack pointers, interrupt base

The 16032 has 32-bit architecture, and has several features intended to support high level languages. There are registers for addressing stack frames and static variables of high level languages, and addressing modes to support communication between software modules with different data spaces, and to handle arrays of 1, 2, 4, or 8-byte objects. There is also support for bit fields and floating point number operations.

Intel 80286

Direct Address Range: 16 Mbytes
Quickest Instruction: 0.2 microseconds (10 MHz clock)
General Registers: 8 (16 bits)
Interrupt Levels: 2

The 80286 is upwards compatible from the 8086/8088 and can run programs written for those machines with little or no change. The differences are in speed, and in the support provided for protected multi-user systems. Memory management and protection facilities are included in the processor chip, making external memory management unnecessary. All instructions are restartable after an exception, making it possible to provide virtual memory of up to 1 gigabyte (1000 megabytes). There is hardware support for rapidly performing a task switch after an interrupt, without intervention by the operating system.

Intel iAPX 432 system (from preliminary information)

The processor of the iAPX 432 system consists of two chips: the 43201 instruction decoder, and the 43202 execution unit. I/O is handled by 43203 interface processors. Data can be handled in units of up to 32 bits, and floating point numbers up to 80 bits long are supported. Addressing is capability-based, allowing protection to be applied to individual data structures. Up to 16 megabytes of real memory can be addressed, while software can use up to a terabyte (1000 gigabytes) of virtual address space. There is built-in support for multiple processors, multitasking, and dynamic storage allocation. The instructions vary in length from a few bits to several hundred bits, and have the unusual property that the start of an instruction does not need to be aligned to any particular memory boundary. Two processors may be coupled pin-to-pin such that one checks the operation of the other, to give high system reliability.

Introduction to the 68000

The rest of this chapter gives an overview of the 68000 as a background to the detailed information in later chapters. Some specific instructions . are mentioned with only a brief description; this is intended more for the reader who has already met assembly language on another computer. Don't worry if these appear mystifying: they are explained fully later.

The memory available to the 68000 is of two different kinds: the internal **registers** (i.e. on the chip), and the external **main memory**. There are 17 registers, of which only 16 are available at any given moment. Eight of them are **data registers** named D0 to D7, and tne others are **address registers** called A0 to A7. Each register contains 32 bits. In many contexts either kind of register may be used, but others demand a specific kind. Any register may be used for operations on **word** (16-bit) and **long word** (32-bit) quantities or for indexed addressing of main memory (see chapter 2). Only data registers may be used for operations on **byte** (8-bit) operands. Only address registers may be used as stack pointers or base registers for addressing main memory. The register A7 is duplicated; which physical register is actually used depends on whether the processor is in supervisor state (see below).

The main memory consists of a number of bytes of storage - how many there are depends on the particular computer system. Each byte has an identifying number, called its **address**. Memory is usually (but not always) arranged so that its bytes have addresses 0, 1, 2, ..., N-2, N-1 where there are N bytes of memory in total. The size of memory which can be directly accessed is very large - . up to 16 million bytes. The 68000 can perform operations on bytes, words, or long words of memory. A word is two consecutive bytes of which the first has an even address. A long word is four consecutive bytes also starting at an even address. The address of a word or long word is the (even) address of its (lowest numbered) first byte.

It is worth noting that a 68000 address can always be represented in 24 bits, so there are 8 spare bits when an address is held in a long word or in a register. This means that addresses are always positive numbers, so there are no catches when two addresses are compared to see which is higher. The fact that addresses can be negative on some other computers which have 16-bit words and 16-bit addresses can be a cause of very obscure errors. In some situations it is very convenient to make use of the eight spare bits, allowing some extra information to be held with a pointer in a long word. This might be an indication of what sort of object the pointer refers to, or simply a flag to say that this is a pointer to a value rather than the value itself. A warning should be issued here: preliminary information from Motorola indicates that they intend to use full 32-bit addresses in future models of the 68000 series, so exploitation of the spare 8 bits may result in programs which are difficult to move to these future models.

As well as holding items of data being manipulated by the computer, the main memory also holds the **instructions** which tell the computer what to do. Each instruction occupies from one to 5 words, consisting of an operation word and between zero and four operand words. The operation word specifies what action is to be performed (and implicitly how many words there are in the whole instruction). The operand words indicate where in the registers or main memory are the items to be manipulated, and where the result should be placed.

Instructions are normally executed one at a time in the order that they occur in memory, rather like performing the steps in a recipe or playing the notes in a piece of written music. There is a special register called the **program counter** which is used to hold the address of the instruction to be obeyed next. Some instructions, called **jumps** or **branches**, upset the normal order, and force execution to continue with the instruction at a specific address. This enables the computer to perform an action repeatedly, or to do different things depending on the values of data items.

There is one other special register, called the **status register** which is used to remember particular things about the state of the computer. The status register has the following layout

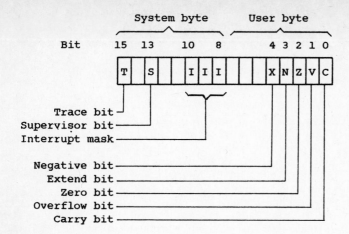

The significance of the bits in the system byte will be explained more fully in chapter 7.

Trace bit   This is set to 1 if the processor is in trace mode, and to 0 otherwise.

Supervisor bit   This is set to 1 if the processor is in supervisor state, and to 0 if the processor is in user state.

Interrupt mask   Indicates which of 7 interrupt levels are enabled.

The user byte contains the five **condition code** flags. These flags are set by certain instructions such as arithmetic or comparison operations to convey information about the result to later instructions. The condition codes have the following meanings

Z   The result was zero

N   The result was negative

V   Overflow occurred during 2s complement arithmetic (i.e. the result is too big to fit in the destination)

C   Carry (or borrow, in subtraction) occurred

X   Extend flag. This is used in multi-length operations (e.g. adding two 64-bit numbers). When it is affected, it will be set the same as the carry flag, but X is altered by fewer instructions than C.

The settings of the condition codes can be tested by the families of instructions Bcc, DBcc, and Scc, which are introduced in chapter 3.

The instructions of the 68000 fall naturally into a small number of groups, and the following chapters each deal with one group. Many instructions are concerned with moving data about – between memory locations, between registers, or between registers and memory. Others perform arithmetic or logical operations, such as adding, or compare data items. The branches and jumps are used to control the order in which program steps are obeyed. A few other instructions do various things, such as stopping the processor obeying instructions, or handling external devices connected to the computer.

Position independent code

Computer programs are often written in such a way that they contain fixed memory addresses specifying the whereabouts of data items or the destinations of jumps. Such a program has to be loaded into a particular place in memory, otherwise it will not work. This may be acceptable on a simple computer system which has only one program in store at once, but it is often much more convenient if a program can be placed anywhere in memory. Such a program is said to be written in **position independent code**.

The instruction set of the 68000 makes it easy to write programs in such a way that they can be loaded anywhere in store. This is because the instructions which cause program jumps specify the destination of the jump in a **relative** rather than an **absolute** way. For example, a branch does not have to be of the form 'go to the instruction at address 5000', but can be specified as 'go to the instruction 192 bytes before this one'. The latter form will work wherever the program is situated in memory. Most computers have branch instructions like this, but usually they only allow a jump up to 128 bytes away from the current instruction, and this is often too little. The 68000 allows jumps up to 32768 bytes away, which will be adequate for virtually any program.

The other aspect of position independence relates to the addressing of data. The rich set of addressing modes of the 68000 (see chapter 2) means that data items can be accessed relative to an address held in a register, so that a program can easily set up its data areas anywhere in memory.

A truly position independent program would be one which could be placed initially anywhere in memory and then moved elsewhere during its execution. Such a program would have to address data relative to the program counter. The 68000 allows one to read data from locations relative to the program counter, but does not allow locations addressed in this way to be altered. This is deliberate, and intended to encourage the clear separation of the areas of memory devoted to program and data, which is good programming practice.

Thus the 68000 makes it straightforward to write programs which can be loaded anywhere in memory, can set up their data areas anywhere, and which can be moved during execution if the data areas stay in the same place.

Debugging aids provided by the chip

The 68000 processor has a number of features to make detection and location of programming errors easier. Some of these are built-in checks for illegal actions, while others are things which the programmer can use to help him debug a program.

The processor has the ability to force a hardware trap when certain things happen. This means that the normal flow of instruction execution is interrupted, the place where it stopped is recorded, and a jump made to a fixed place in memory. This place should contain a piece of program which can take suitable action, for instance printing out an error message telling the user what happened, and asking him whether or not he wants to allow his program to continue. If he does, then a jump can be made back to the place where execution stopped.

The following events cause a trap to occur:

- Access to a word or long word with an odd address
- Encountering an unimplemented or illegal instruction
- Attempt to access memory which does not exist
- Dividing a number by zero
- Spurious interrupt from a peripheral device

Certain instructions can cause traps. The TRAPV instruction causes a trap if the last arithmetic operation overflowed. It can thus be included after each arithmetic operation in the program if this check is desired. Similarly, the CHK instruction will trap if the value in a register is greater than a specified number. This can be included to check that a memory access is within a particular region of data.

The instruction TRAP always causes a trap. It can be inserted at strategic points in a program to cause it to stop so that the contents of registers and memory can be inspected, allowing the operation of the program to be checked in stages.

A final debugging aid is a means whereby a program can be executed one instruction at a time, providing a very powerful way of detecting exactly where a fault occurs. This is achieved by setting one of the bits in the status register, putting the machine into trace mode. In this mode, a trap is taken after each instruction is obeyed. With the help of a suitable debugging program to intercept this trap, the user can step through critical regions of his program to check its operation in detail. This is a facility which it can be very difficult to provide on a computer without a trace mode.

The use of traps in debugging is illustrated in chapter 7.

Support for high level languages

The 68000 has been designed in the knowledge that many of its users will not want to program it in assembly code, but will instead wish to use one of the many high level computer languages, such as FORTRAN, Pascal, or Algol68. A high level language program is written in a form which is much closer to ordinary English than assembly language. This means that programs can be written much more quickly and easily than in assembly code, and mistakes in them are usually easier to find. Such programs can also have the advantage of being portable. That is, they will work on any machine on which the language is available; assembly language programs can run only on the type of computer for which they were written.

A program called a compiler is used to translate commands written in a high level language into machine code, the instructions which the computer understands. The machine code produced by a compiler is usually of rather poor quality compared to that which a human could write. It tends to do things in ways which take more instructions than actually necessary, meaning that code from a compiler occupies more memory and runs more slowly than that written by a human. However, now that computing power and memory are comparatively cheap, it is quite acceptable to waste them in order to save human effort.

The 68000 has features intended to simplify the writing of compilers for high level languages, and to enable them to produce reasonably efficient code. The fact that the machine has 16 all purpose registers is helpful, as it means that frequently used pointers and values can be kept in registers all the time, so that there will not be so much code generated just to shuffle things around between memory and registers. The regular and consistent structure of the instructions and address modes simplifies the part of the compiler concerned with actually generating the machine code. Most instructions can operate on objects of three different sizes and employ any of the address modes. The ability to address directly a large amount of memory simplifies the organisation of storage for a language.

Several instructions are included specifically for high level languages. Programs in such languages are usually written as separate modules or routines which are combined to form the complete program. When compiling one module, the compiler does not know from where in the program it will be used, and hence does not know which machine registers and which areas of memory can safely be used within the module. The problem of deciding which registers are available is most easily solved by saving the contents of some registers when the module is entered, and restoring them all again when it is left. The instruction MOVEM does just this, copying from a specified set of registers to memory or back again. It is very flexible, being able to save or restore any arbitrary group of registers.

The instructions LINK and UNLK allow each program module called to allocate itself a private area of storage from a stack (see chapter 4). The effect of LINK is to save a pointer to the current workspace, and to reserve a new one of specified size. UNLK inverts the operation, releasing the space allocated and restoring the pointer to the old one.

The instructions mentioned in the section on debugging aids, such as CHK and TRAPV, can also be employed to good effect in compiled code so that errors such as arithmetic overflow, or an attempt to use memory outside a particular data structure, can be detected immediately. Being single instructions, the inclusion of such checks does not greatly slow down execution of the program. A compiler can reliably include such instructions at every appropriate place – something it would be difficult for a human to do.

Operating system support

A bare computer is an object which is rather difficult to use. The only thing it can do is to execute instructions coded in its own machine language. For this reason, it is normal always to run a program to make the machine easier to use. Such a program is called an operating system; a very simple operating system is sometimes called a monitor.

A typical operating system will handle all the peripheral devices attached to the computer, interpret commands typed by the user at the terminal, and manage the disc storage to provide files with names convenient for humans. It may allow several programs to be run apparently at the same time, in fact by switching between them at a rapid rate. It will also handle certain errors in a running program, print an informatory message for the user, and provide him with commands for inspecting his program in store and the contents of the registers.

The 68000 has many features which are necessary or helpful in supporting an operating system. It gives the operating system the means to protect itself from damage caused by the programs it runs, and to maintain control over those programs. This is achieved by using the two processor modes: supervisor mode and user mode. The operating system runs in supervisor mode, and switches the processor to user mode before allowing any other program to run. Several critical instructions are privileged and may not be executed in user mode. The processor chip has an output line which indicates the mode during each access to memory or peripherals, making it possible to attach hardware so that the peripherals and certain areas of memory are available only in supervisor mode. Thus the operating system can protect the store holding its code and private workspace, and be sure that it is the only program with access to the peripherals. It must be possible to ensure that no user program can set supervisor mode, but that it can call operating system routines and have them run in that mode. The first is achieved because the instructions which can change mode are privileged. The second is achieved through the TRAP instruction (see chapter 7), which can simultaneously cause a jump and alter the mode.

The 68000 has vectored interrupts and traps (see chapter 7): this allows each peripheral device to signal to the processor, causing a direct jump to an appropriate piece of code to deal with that device, thus simplifying the operating system. The provision of several levels of interrupt makes it possible to organise the processing of interrupt signals from different devices such that the most urgent ones get dealt with first.

The MOVEM instruction is useful again in operating systems. When an interrupt or trap occurs, there is an immediate jump to some point in the operating system; the code there must save the contents of any registers which it wishes to use itself. Another special instruction is MOVEP, provided specifically to simplify the transfer of data to peripheral devices.

When two programs are being run in parallel, it will sometimes be necessary to allow one of them to claim exclusive access to some resource (e.g. a device or area of store). This is most simply done by having a flag byte in memory which indicates whether the resource is free. The resource is claimed by waiting until the flag is free and then setting it. However, the actions of inspecting and setting the flag must be performed as an indivisible operation, otherwise two programs could both find the flag free, and both claim the resource. The test and set (TAS) instruction is provided for just this purpose. It can also be used for interlocks between programs running in several processors sharing the same memory, because the processor retains control of the memory for the whole TAS instruction. This is sometimes called a read–modify–write cycle.

The 68000 processor includes bus arbitration logic, to allow its bus (main communication cable) to be shared between all the devices connected to it. This includes the memory, terminal, discs, and other processors. Intelligent devices can get at the memory directly, without having to interrupt the processor. Such an arrangement is called **direct memory access** (DMA). For instance, the processor could ask a disc device to transfer some data from the disc to memory. The device could do the transfer using DMA, interrupting only when it had finished, and leaving the processor free to execute some more program in the meantime.

Some typical applications

The 68000 is as yet still too expensive to be used in equipment which does not actually need its speed or large memory capacity; such applications are likely to remain the domain of the inexpensive 8-bit microprocessors. Its use lies in more demanding situations, such as computer terminals, graphics workstations, word processors and medical equipment. As a general purpose computer, it is a serious rival to minicomputers of all sizes. The large address space means that it can make a powerful personal computer which can run programs which previously could only run on a mainframe machine. It can also be used to support several users at once, although in this case some memory mapping hardware is required to isolate one user from another.

Other processors in the 68000 series

The 68000 is just the first model in a range of similar processors. This section briefly describes the three other models which had been announced at the time of writing: the 68008, 68010, and 68020.

The 68008 is simply the 68000 with an 8-bit (rather than 16-bit) external data bus. It enables the processor to be used with 8-bit support chips, giving some reduction in circuit complexity and cost, at the expense of reduced execution speed.

The 68010 is very similar to the 68000, but with some modifications to improve operating system support and to make it faster. There is a new internal register, called the Vector Base Register, which holds the address of the base of the interrupt vectors (see chapter 7). It is set to zero by default (for compatability with the 68000), but can be altered, allowing different operating system processes to handle their own traps in a straightforward way.

A number of changes have been made to the information stored on the stack after an exception. In particular this will enable an instruction which caused a bus error to be restarted. This allows the implementation of a system with virtual memory in which programs appear to have access to more memory than is physically available. The operating system ensures that those sections of virtual memory actually in use at any moment are copied into real memory, while the rest is held on backing store such as a disc. The translation of virtual addresses into real addresses is arranged in such a way that an attempt to use a location which has not been copied into real memory will cause a bus error. The operating system responds to the bus error by fetching the relevant part of the virtual address space into real store, and then resuming execution with the instruction that caused the bus error.

The 68010 has two new instructions: MOVEC and MOVES. MOVEC is used for access to various control registers, including the Vector Base Pointer. MOVES allows reading and writing of the address spaces which would normally be inaccessible. Data accesses are normally made to the User Data or Supervisor Data address spaces, according to the current privilege level. However, there are two 3-bit function code registers (one for source and one for destination) which can be set by MOVEC, so that a program running in supervisor state can then use MOVES to read or write locations in the Supervisor Program, User Program, or User Data address spaces.

Various instructions execute more quickly in the 68010 than in the 68000, including the 32-bit arithmetic and logical operations, CLR, Scc, and MOVE SR. Also, the bus error timings have been relaxed, so there is no execution speed penalty for having error detection on memory.

The 68020 processor contains all the new features of the 68010, plus others to increase support for 32-bit operations. It has a full 32-bit external data bus, 32-bit offsets in branch instructions, and 32-bit displacements in indexed addressing modes. The instructions CHK, LINK, UNLK, MUL, and DIV can take 32-bit operands. An extra addressing mode is available, allowing indexed addressing with two levels of indirection.

The 68020 has an instruction cache, enabling small loops to run very fast as the instructions do not have to be repeatedly fetched from memory. It also has a complete coprocessor interface, allowing the instruction set to be extended by the addition of other chips (e.g. to provide floating point arithmetic).

There are several new instructions available on the 68020. These include an instruction for moving blocks of data between address spaces, more sophisticated entry and exit operations for procedure calls in high level languages, and MOVEF for moving various sized bit fields. The range of instructions for packed decimal data is extended by PACK and UNPK, which convert between characters and decimal numbers.

Chapter 2

Assembler syntax and addressing modes

This chapter provides the necessary background for the introduction of the various machine instructions in later chapters. It explains the assembler syntax – that is, the way a program is written down – and the addressing modes, which are the different ways in which instructions locate the data on which they are to act.

Assembler syntax

The only language which the computer itself understands is **machine code**, which can be considered as just a pattern of bits, or as a list of numbers, in its memory. A program in this form is rather hard for a human either to understand or to write. Consequently, programs are more usually written in **assembly language**, which directly corresponds to the machine code, but makes use of mnemonic names for instructions and registers. It also allows the programmer to use symbolic names for addresses within the program, and for other values. A program called an **assembler** is used to translate from the assembly language into machine language. The form of the assembly language presented below is the same as that used by Motorola and accepted by their assemblers. If you are using an assembler from another source, you may have to use a variant of the language: consult your manual to find out if there are any differences.

A program is composed of a series of steps called **instructions**. Each instruction is written as one line of assembly language. The instruction itself has a mnemonic name of 3, 4, or 5 letters, and for some instructions the name is all that need be written on the line. An example is

      NOP

which is an instruction that does nothing at all! (Such an instruction is not completely pointless: it can be useful when debugging as a replacement for some unwanted instruction, and can also be used when a very short delay is required.)

Note that the name has been written indented from the left hand margin; the reason for this will be made clear below.

However, for most instructions, the name alone is not sufficient, as we must also specify where in the registers or memory are the data on which they are to operate. This is done by putting the operand after the name (with one or more spaces in between), as in

```
CLR     D3
```

which clears to zero the least significant 16 bits of data register 3. If there are two operands, then they are separated by a comma (but no spaces). The left hand operand is usually the **source** from which a value is read, while the right hand one is the **destination**, in which the result is placed. It is important to note that the operands are written in this order, particularly if you are used to an assembly language for another computer which works the other way round. A simple example is

```
MOVE    D1,D4
```

which just copies the least significant 16 bits from data register 1 to register 4 (without affecting the rest of either).

The 68000 has the useful feature that many of its instructions can work on data of three different sizes: byte (8 bits), word (16 bits), or long word (32 bits). To indicate which length is required, the suffix '.B', '.W', or '.L' is added to the name; '.W' is assumed if no suffix is added. Thus, the above instruction is the same as

```
MOVE.W  D1,D4
```

and to copy all 32 bits of the register, we would write

```
MOVE.L  D1,D4
```

Similarly, to clear just the least significant 8 bits of a register, we would say

```
CLR.B   D3
```

It is a good idea to get into the habit of always using the length suffix (i.e. not missing off the optional '.W'), as a common programming error on the 68000 is using the word form of an instruction by mistake. This can cause obscure faults in a program, which can be difficult to track down. You are much less likely to make this mistake if you always put in the qualifier.

Anything else on the line after the instruction and its operands (if any) is ignored by the assembler. This allows the insertion of comments in the program in order to make it more easily understood by a human reader. If a line starts with a star, then the whole line is treated as a comment.

```
* This whole line is a comment
        CLR.L   D3              A comment after an instruction
```

The extensive use of comments in programs is strongly recommended. Although it may seem tedious to include them when the program is being written, they make it very much easier for someone other than the author to understand it, or for the author himself to modify it some time after he originally wrote it.

In the examples above, instruction names have been written indented from the left hand margin. If a line does not start with a space, then the first item is taken to be a label, which is a symbolic name for the memory address of the instruction on that line. The name of a label may be any word which starts with a letter and contains just letters and digits. (In practice, most assemblers allow some other characters to be used in names. In the examples in this book, we have used the underline character '_' to improve the readability of names.) The assembler remembers the label and the address which it refers to, and the label may be used elsewhere in the program to refer to that address. This is particularly useful with jump instructions, which cause execution to continue at a specified address.

```
CLRD3    CLR.L   D3              Labelled instruction
  :
  :
         JMP     CLRD3           Jump to instruction labelled CLRD3
```

A label may also be written indented from the margin, by putting a colon after its name

```
 CLRD3: CLR.L   D3
```

Making use of labels in this way relieves us of having to know the actual address of the CLR instruction, and means that we do not have to alter the JMP instruction every time modifications to the rest of the program cause this address to change.

Assembler directives

As well as instructions and comments, the assembler also accepts directives, which are commands to the assembler itself. They are written in the same way as instructions, but (with the exception of DC and DS) do not cause any code to be generated. The only directives described here are a few basic ones which are likely to be available in the same form in most 68000 assemblers. Most assemblers will have other directives as well, to control things such as layout of the assembly listing, format of object module produced, and to provide facilities for conditional assembly and macros.

An example of a directive is EQU, which equates a symbolic name to a value (rather like the way a label is a name for an address). For example

```
SIZE    EQU     100
```

sets up SIZE as a name for the value 100. Wherever 'SIZE' is used in the program, the assembler will act as if '100' had been written instead. This can be useful in several ways. If several parts of the program depend on this value, it is much easier to alter if SIZE is defined once at the beginning and used throughout, rather than if '100' is written explicitly in several places. It can also make a program more comprehensible to human readers if mnemonic names are used for numbers.

Memory in the 68000 is thought of as an array of 8-bit **bytes**, numbered 0, 1, 2, upwards. The number of a memory byte is called its **address**. There are two directives for controlling the location in memory of the assembled code. One is ORG, which specifies a particular address for the origin (i.e. first instruction). The sequence

```
        ORG     1024
START   CLR.L   D3
        :
        :
```

will cause the assembler to produce the code assuming that it will be placed at address 1024 onwards. Thus the label START will have value 1024. The assembled code will be marked with this address so that it can be loaded at the correct position. Code starting with ORG is called **absolute** code, because its address is fixed; labels within it are said to be absolute symbols. A program which includes an ORG is unlikely to be position independent, as it will contain explicit references to particular addresses. ORG has an alternative form, ORG.L, which affects the assembly of the absolute addressing mode (see below).

It is often convenient to be able to write numbers in a program in hexadecimal (base 16), or 'hex', notation instead of in decimal. The digits used are 0 to 9, and then A to F representing 10 to 15. The assembler accepts hexadecimal numbers starting with a dollar character. Thus

```
        ORG     $400
```

is the same as ORG 1024 (= 4*256 + 0*16 + 0*1). Throughout this book, '$' is used to introduce hexadecimal numbers.

The complementary directive to ORG is RORG, which indicates that the program is **relocatable**, meaning that it may be placed anywhere in memory. RORG also takes an argument, but this should normally be zero. If we alter the above program fragment to

```
        RORG    0
START   CLR.L   D3
        :
        :
```

then the value of START will not be known to the assembler. START will be given the value zero (because that is its offset from the beginning of the section) and the fact that it is relocatable will be noted. Labels such as START are examples of **relocatable symbols** – symbols whose value will not be known until the program is loaded into memory. Wherever a relocatable symbol is used, the assembler will try to produce the code in a position independent way. Thus, in

```
        RORG    0
START   CLR.L   D3
        :
        :
        JMP     START
```

the JMP instruction will be coded as 'jump to the instruction X bytes before here', where X is calculated by the assembler. If a relocatable value is used in such a way that position independent code cannot be produced, then the assembler will include with the code a list of those words within it whose values must be filled in when the program is actually placed in store. It is not until then that those values can be known. This list is called the **relocation information**.

Two directives are available for reserving and initialising memory locations. The DS (Define Storage) directive is used to reserve an area of memory. It takes a suffix indicating the size of the locations, and an operand which says how many such locations are to be reserved. Examples are

```
BUFFER  DS.B    80          Reserve 80 bytes of memory
        DS.W    $20         Reserve 32 words
        DS      $20         Reserve 32 words
        DS.L    3           Reserve 3 long words
```

The memory reserved is not initialised to any particular value. Unless the size specifier is '.B', then the space is aligned to a word boundary, so 'DS.W 0' can be used just to force word alignment. If the DS directive is labelled, then the label will refer to the address of the first location reserved (after any alignment).

The DC (Define Constant) directive is used to assemble particular values into memory locations. It takes the usual three size specifiers, and one or more operands separated by commas. If the size specifier is not '.B', then alignment to a word boundary is forced as for DS. The operands may be numbers, expressions, or a string of characters enclosed in single quotes. A string of characters after DC is treated specially: it is not taken to be a character constant (see "Expressions" below), but instead one byte is assembled for each character. If DC.W or DC.L is used, the final word or long word is padded with zero bytes if necessary.

```
MESSAGE DC.B    'Hello'     5 bytes containing the
*                           codes for 'H', 'e', etc.
        DC.L    'Hello'     8 bytes are assembled:
*                           the last 3 hold zeros.
        DC.W    10,20,30    3 words are assembled
        DC.L    $FF,99      2 long words are assembled
```

The directive END is used simply to mark the end of an assembler program. The last line of any program should be

```
        END
```

Summary of assembler directives

Directive			Function
[label]	DC.s	exp,exp,..	Assemble values of size s
[label]	DS.s	n	Reserve n locations of size s
	END		End of source program
symbol	EQU	value	Equate symbol to value
	ORG	address	Set origin of absolute section
	RORG	address	Set origin of relocatable section

Summary of assembler syntax

There are three main types of assembler line: comment lines, instruction lines, and directive lines. A comment line starts with an asterisk; any characters may appear on the rest of the line.

```
* This is a comment line
```

An instruction line has the general form

```
label   opcode  operand(s)   comment
```

Each field is separated from the next by at least one space, and the label, opcode and operand fields may not contain embedded spaces (except inside quoted character strings). The label and comment are always optional. The opcode field consists of an instruction name, optionally followed by a length qualifier ('.B', '.W', '.L', or '.S'). The number of operands is determined by the instruction opcode. If no operands are expected, then the assembler will treat anything after the opcode field as comment. If there are two operands, then they should be separated by a comma (but no spaces).

A directive line has the general form

```
label   directive argument(s) comment
```

The label field is not allowed for some directives, and is compulsory for others. If there are two or more arguments, they should be separated by commas.

Expressions

As we have seen above, in most places where you might write a number, you can write a symbol representing that number. In fact, we can replace a number by an arithmetic expression containing symbols and numbers. A variety of arithmetic operators are available, including +, −, * (multiply), and / (divide). We can write things like

```
DAYHRS  EQU    24             Hours in a day
DAYMINS EQU    DAYHRS*60      Minutes in a day
DAYSECS EQU    DAYMINS*60     Seconds in a day
```

The value is worked out using integer arithmetic, so all results are whole numbers. This matters only for division, where the result is rounded down so, for example, 7/3 is 2.

Numbers may be written in decimal or hexadecimal (preceded by a '$'). Another way of specifying a number is as a character constant. This consists of between one and four characters enclosed in single quotes, and its value is that of a long word with the specified characters in the rightmost (least significant) byte positions, and zeros on the left. Character constants are most useful for single characters, and should be used in preference to the numerical code for a character to improve readability. For example

```
CHARZ   EQU    'Z'            Code for letter Z
CASEDIFF EQU   'A'-'a'        Difference between codes
*                             for upper and lower case
*                             forms of same letter
```

We have seen above that symbols are of two types: absolute and relocatable. There are no problems in arithmetic with absolute symbols, as they are just like numbers. However, there are restrictions on what you can do with relocatable symbols and still produce a meaningful result. The basic rule is that the answer must either be absolute, or relocatable in the same way as the original symbols. Thus multiplication or division involving relocatable quantities is not allowed, nor is addition of two relocatable values. A constant may be added to or subtracted from a relocatable value, giving a relocatable result (which is just the address of a different point in the same relocatable section). We could write

```
        RORG   0              Relocatable section
START   CLR.L  D3             This instruction is two bytes long
        CLR.L  D4
        :
        :
        JMP    START+2        Jump to second CLR.L above
```

though it would be better practice to put a label on the instruction we actually want to jump to.

It is illegal to subtract a relocatable number from an absolute one, but perfectly all right to subtract one relocatable number from another. The result is an absolute number, as it represents the distance apart of two points in a program, which will be the same wherever it happens to be placed in memory. In the program

```
        RORG   0              Relocatable section
PSTART  MOVE.L PEND-PSTART,D0 Set D0 to program length
        :
        :
PEND
```

the first instruction moves the length (in bytes) of the whole program into D0. Note that we have used a label on a line by itself: its value is the address of the byte after the last one assembled.

The above rules can be summarised in a table:

Expression	Result
relocatable*anything	(illegal)
relocatable/anything	(illegal)
relocatable+absolute	relocatable
relocatable−absolute	relocatable
relocatable−relocatable	absolute
absolute−relocatable	(illegal)

Addressing modes

Most of the instructions of the 68000 can accept their operands in a variety of forms. They can be in registers, in memory locations addressed by a variety of methods, or even included in the instruction itself. Because the instruction set is organised in such a regular way, it is possible to describe the various addressing modes independently of the instructions. The term used to describe an operand which can be expressed in any (or almost any) of the addressing modes is an **effective address**.

Register direct addressing

Operand data may be held in one of the data registers or one of the address registers. The register name is written as Dn or An, where n is a digit from 0 to 7. For example

```
MOVE.L   A7,D5
```

copies all 32 bits of address register 7 into data register 5. If the length is 'word', only the least significant 16 bits of the register are read or altered. Length code 'byte' may not be used with address registers; with data registers only the bottom 8 bits are affected.

Absolute addressing

An operand in memory may be located by giving the absolute address of its first (most significant) byte. The operand is written simply as a number, or as a label or other symbol representing the number. To clear the byte at location 1000 (hex), we could write

```
CLR.B    $1000
```

There are in fact two forms of this addressing mode, as the absolute address can be held as a 16-bit or a 32-bit number in the instruction. In the short form, the 16-bit address is **sign-extended** to 32 bits before it is used. This means that the most significant bit of the 16-bit number is copied to the most significant 16 bits of the address. Thus, the short form can be used to address the bottom 32K bytes of memory, and a region of up to 32K at the top of memory, but nowhere in between. For backward references, the assembler can always choose the correct length, as it already knows the address of the location being referred to. A length qualifier may be added to the ORG directive in order to control which form of this addressing mode will be chosen for forward references: ORG.L asks for the long mode, while ORG asks for the short one. What this means in practice is that, if a program in absolute code extends to addresses above 32K (=$8000), then ORG.L must be used in order to inform the assembler that forward references may need more than 16 bits.

These address calculations can be represented diagramatically (with '<<<' used to indicate sign extension).

Short Absolute Mode

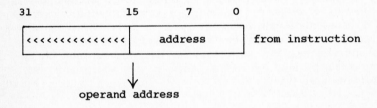

Long Absolute Mode

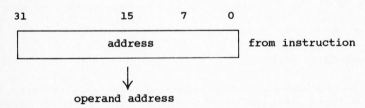

Relative addressing

Two modes allow memory to be addressed relative to the current value of the program counter (PC). This is used mainly for jumps in position independent code, but can also be used to read constants built into the program. A location addressed in this way may not be written to: this is to encourage the writing of **pure code**. This is code which does not alter itself as it runs, and so can be executed again with the same effect, or indeed executed as part of several programs running simultaneously. Pure code is said to be **re-entrant**, meaning that it is always available to be used again. A lower level of 'purity' is code which is **serially reusable**, meaning that it can be used again once it has finished, but may not be in its proper state all the time that it is running.

In the simpler of the two relative addressing modes, the memory address is calculated as the sum of the current program counter and a 16-bit displacement value. During the execution of an instruction, the value of the program counter is two more than the address of the start of the instruction. The displacement is treated as a signed 16-bit number, so it is possible to represent addresses from instruction-32766 to instruction+32769 in this way.

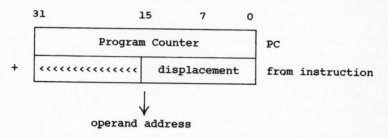

This mode can be requested by writing the operand address as an offset from the start of the current instruction. The symbol '*' is available to refer to the current location. We can thus write things like

```
JMP       *+10           Jump to the instruction 10 bytes on
```

but it is not advisable to do so, as firstly we must calculate the offset ourselves, and secondly, remember to alter it if any instructions are inserted in between. It is easier and safer to use labels.

The assembler will generate this mode automatically if a reference is made in a relocatable section to a relocatable symbol defined in the same section. If we write

```
        RORG    0
START   CLR.L   D3
        :
        :
        JMP     START
```

then the assembler will use the program counter with displacement mode for the JMP instruction.

The other program counter relative mode is similar, but the contents of a register are also added in when calculating the address. Such a register is called an **index** register, and may be any of the 16 registers. How much of the index register is significant is indicated by suffixing the register name with '.W' (the default) or '.L'. The displacement value in this mode is only 8 bits long, but signed, so can modify the PC value by −128 to +127.

Long form

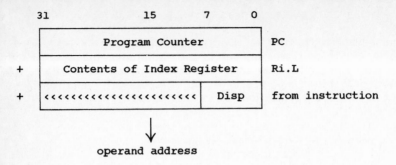

operand address

Word form

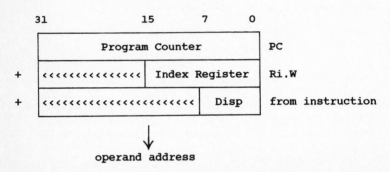

operand address

The most common use of this mode is when jumping to one of several locations, when the actual one wanted has been decided earlier in the program. This mode is chosen when a relocatable symbol is followed by the name of a (data or address) register in brackets. For example

```
         RORG    0
           :                    Code which calculates which routine
           :                    should be executed, and places
           :                    0, 4, 8, or 12 in A0 accordingly.
           :                    (We know each JMP is 4 bytes long.)
*
         JMP     JTABLE(A0)     Jump to appropriate JMP instruction
*
JTABLE   JMP     ROUTINEA       Executed if A0 contains  0
         JMP     ROUTINEB       Executed if A0 contains  4
         JMP     ROUTINEC       Executed if A0 contains  8
         JMP     ROUTINED       Executed if A0 contains 12
```

This mode has two different forms, using either 16 or 32 bits of the index register

```
         JMP     JTABLE(A0.W) is the same as in the example above.
*                             Only the bottom 16 bits of A0 used
*                             treated as a 16-bit signed number.
         JMP     JTABLE(A0.L) uses all 32 bits of A0.
```

Address register indirect

There are five addressing modes based on an operand address held in one of the address registers. This is called **indirect** addressing because the register is not itself the operand, but only points at the operand in memory.

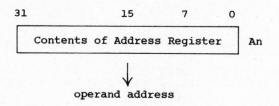

The simplest of these modes is specified by writing the name of the address register in brackets, as in

        CLR.B   (A2)

which clears the byte whose address is in A2.

Register indirect with displacement

The address in an address register can be modified by the addition of a signed 16-bit displacement value.

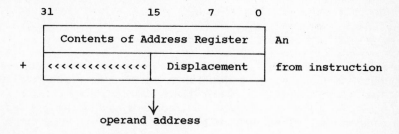

Suppose that A2 contains 50000:

        CLR.B   100(A2)   Clears byte at 50100
        CLR.B   -32000(A2)   Clears byte at 18000

This mode is used when an address register points at some data structure which contains items at fixed offsets that we want to access individually.

Register indirect with displacement and index

This is similar to the last mode, except that the contents of another register are added in, and the displacement value is only 8 bits in size.

Long form

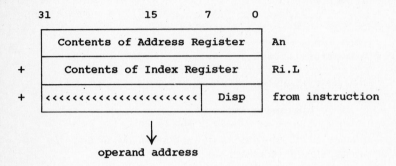

Word form

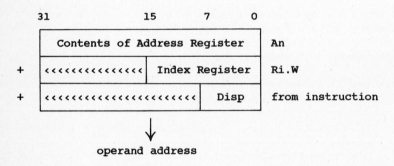

The index register may be any of the 16 registers; how much of it is significant is indicated by suffixing the register name with '.W' (the default) or '.L'.

Suppose A0 contains $230000, A1 contains $FFFC (= −4 as a 16-bit number) and A2 contains $20. Then

```
CLR.B    $10(A0,A2)    clears byte $230030
CLR.B    $10(A0,A2.W)    "      "   $230030
CLR.B    $10(A0,A2.L)    "      "   $230030
CLR.B    $10(A2,A0.L)    "      "   $230030
CLR.B    $10(A2,A0.W)    "      "       $30
CLR.B    $10(A0,A1.W)    "      "   $23000C
CLT.B    $10(A0,A1.L)    "      "   $24000C
```

The use of this mode allows access to calculated offsets in a data structure whose address is held in a register.

Register Indirect with predecrement or postincrement

Two variants of the basic address register indirect mode are included to simplify the management of stacks (see chapter 4). Both of these refer to a location whose address is in a register, and alter the register's contents so that it points to an adjacent location.
The predecrement mode is written −(An). Its effect is to reduce the value in An by one, two, or four, depending on whether the operand size of the instruction is byte, word, or long, and then to access the location addressed by the adjusted An.

Predecrement mode

Contents of An are decremented by 1, 2, or 4.

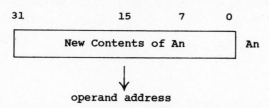

Thus, if A1, A2, and A3 each contain 1000, then

```
    CLR.B   -(A1)       sets A1 to 999,
*                       and clears the byte at 999
    CLR.W   -(A2)       sets A2 to 998,
*                       and clears the word at 998
    CLR.L   -(A3)       sets A3 to 996,
*                       ands clears the long word at 996
```

The postincrement mode is written (An)+ and is the exact opposite. The access is made to the location originally addressed by An, and then the value in An is increased by one, two, or four.

Postincrement mode

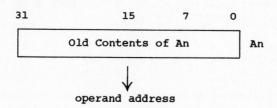

Contents of An are then incremented by 1, 2, or 4.

If A1 contains 1000, then

```
    CLR.W   (A1)+       clears the word at 1000,
*                       and then sets A1 to 1002
```

Take care if you choose to use A7 in either of these modes. This register is special in that the hardware uses it automatically in some situations (interrupts, exceptions, and subroutine calls), and expects it always to contain an even address. Because of this, these two modes will adjust the value of A7 by two, not one, in a byte-size instruction, to keep its value even.

Immediate data

This addressing mode allows the operand value to be held in the instruction itself, and is allowed for source operands only. The data value is written #number, and the length to which it is stored depends on the data size of the instruction. Thus

```
MOVE.B  #$FF,D0
```

inserts the hex number FF into the low byte of D0, while

```
MOVE.L  #$56789ABC,D0
```

sets the whole of D0 to 56789ABC (hex).

A common programming mistake, and one that is not necessarily detected quickly, is to miss off the '#' in an immediate operand. If we had written

```
MOVE.B  $FE,D0
```

by accident, then the result would be to load the contents of memory location $FE, instead of the value $FE, into D0.

Some instructions have a so-called 'quick' variant which allows a small immediate operand to be included in the instruction. The syntax is as for the normal immediate mode. An example is the MOVEQ instruction, which takes an 8-bit signed operand

```
MOVEQ   #-3,D7      Set D7 to -3 (size is Long)
```

There are similar instructions for adding or subtracting a number between 1 and 8. For example

```
ADDQ.L  #4,A2
SUBQ.B  #1,(A1)
```

Summary of addressing modes

The table below provides a brief summary of the addressing modes described above.

Mode	Syntax	Effective Address
Data Register	Dn	EA = Dn
Address Register	An	EA = An
Absolute Address	number or ASYMB	EA = fixed number (16 or 32 bits)
PC Relative	RSYMB	EA = [PC] + d16
PC Rel. with Index	RSYMB(Ri)	EA = [PC] + [Ri] + d8
Register Indirect	(An)	EA = [An]
R.I. with Offset	d16(An)	EA = [An] + d16
R.I. Index & Offset	d8(An,Ri)	EA = [An] + [Ri] + d8
Predecrement R.I.	-(An)	[An] := [An] - N; EA = [An]
Postincrement R.I.	(An)+	EA = [An]; [An] := [An] + N
Immediate Data	#number or #ASYMB	Operand in instruction

Explanation of symbols:

EA = Effective Address	Ri = any A or D register
Dn = Data Register	An = Address Register
d8 = 8-bit displacement	d16 = 16-bit displacement
PC = Program Counter	N = 1, 2, or 4 (according to size)
[] = 'contents of'	:= = 'becomes'
ASYMB = Absolute Symbol	RSYMB = Relocatable Symbol

Implicit addressing

This is not a general addressing mode like the ones above, but is another way of locating an operand. Implicit reference to operands occurs in a few instructions which automatically make use of particular machine registers or stack locations. Registers whose use can be implicit are the program counter (PC), the processor status register (SR), and the stack pointer registers (SP) which are the two incarnations of address register 7 (USP and SSP).

   An example of implicit addressing which we have already seen is the JMP instruction, which modifies the program counter in order to effect the jump.

Categories of effective address

In many instructions where an operand is specified as an effective address, not all of the above addressing modes are allowed. The forbidden ones may be nonsensical or just undesirable. Consider the following (illegal) instructions:

```
JMP     D6            Jump to a register
JMP     -(A5)         Decrement A5 by 1, 2, or 4?
MOVE    D4,#77        Copy D4 into constant 77
```

In order that the restrictions on any operand can be expressed concisely, the various address modes are put into four overlapping categories: **data** references, **memory** references, **alterable** operands, and **control** references. Thus, we may talk about 'control addressing modes', 'data alterable addressing modes', and so on.

Data operands include everything except the contents of address registers, while memory operands are anything not held in either sort of register. An operand is alterable if it may be written to. Control operands are those which can be used to indicate the destination of a jump.

The categories to which each mode belongs are summarised in the table below.

Mode	Data	Memory	Control	Alterable
Dn	*			*
An				*
PC relative	*	*	*	
PCR + index	*	*	*	
(An)	*	*	*	*
d16(An)	*	*	*	*
d8(An,Ri)	*	*	*	*
-(An)	*	*		*
(An)+	*	*		*
Absolute	*	*	*	*
#data	*	*		

Chapter 3

Moving and comparing data

The most elementary instruction in the 68000 instruction set is called MOVE. Its purpose is simply to move information from one part of the computer system to another. Unlike many other computers, there is no distinction within the 68000 between moving data in to or out of registers. It is also possible to move data from one memory location to another directly without having to use an intermediate register.

Simple data movement

There are a number of variants on the basic MOVE instruction which we shall come to later. Consider first a simple program to fill memory with data. The immediate address mode may be used for the source, while the absolute form can be used for the destination. Thus

```
        MOVE.B  #123,BYTELOC
```

will set the single byte of memory defined by the label BYTELOC to contain the decimal number 123.

  We could instead use a register as the destination, and use the form

```
        MOVE.L  #123,D1
```

which sets the data register D1 to contain the value 123. Notice that in this case we have used the long form of the instruction rather than the byte form. The data registers are 32 bits wide, and so we have set the entire register to the value 123. If we use any other form of the MOVE instruction, such as

```
        MOVE.B  #123,D1
```

then the effect is simply to set the low order byte to the value 123. The rest of the register D1 is left unchanged in this case. Although this effect is often useful, it is also an easy mistake to accidentally move a byte into a register without first ensuring that the register is empty. This is particularly likely when moving a byte of data from memory into a register. The instruction

```
MOVE.B  BYTELOC,D1
```

does not set register D1 to the byte value stored in location BYTELOC. Instead it slots the byte value of BYTELOC into the bottom 8 bits of D1. Of course if subsequent instructions acting on the value stored in D1 are only byte length instructions then everything will work perfectly. But beware of using the instruction in cases such as

```
MOVE.B  BYTELOC,D1
MOVE.L  D1,LONGLOC
```

which will set the 32 bit value at LONGLOC to the top 24 bits of the previous value of D1, and the byte at LONGLOC+3 to the value stored at BYTELOC.

Another popular trap to fall into is to forget that a byte length instruction alters the bottom 8 bits of a register, but the top 8 bits of a memory location. A reference to store starts using it from the address specified, so that moving a byte to LONGLOC will alter a single byte at that location.

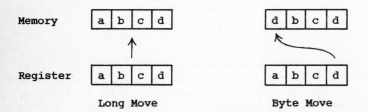

Memory / Register

Long Move   Byte Move

If the word form of the instruction is used then two bytes will be written, at locations LONGLOC and LONGLOC+1. But placing a word into a register using the word form of the instruction and then storing the register at LONGLOC using the long form will alter four bytes from LONGLOC to LONGLOC+3; the top two bytes will contain the previous value of the register and the bottom two bytes will be the word value moved into it.

Any data alterable address mode may be used as the destination of a MOVE operation, and any address mode can be used as the source, with one exception. This is when the byte sized version of the instruction is used, and in this case an address register may not be used as the source.

When a MOVE instruction is used to move data into memory or into a data register, the condition codes in the status register are set accordingly. If the data value moved was zero then the Z bit in the status register is set, otherwise it is cleared. If the value was negative then the N bit is set, otherwise it is cleared. The V bit, which is used to indicate overflow, and the C bit, normally set when a carry has occurred, are both cleared. The X bit is used to remember that a carry has occurred at the last arithmetic instruction, and so this status bit is unchanged.

These changes to the status register do not take place when a value is moved into an address register. This is because it is useful to adjust the value of an address register used as an index without altering the condition codes which might be tested in a subsequent instruction. In order to remind you of the difference, a separate instruction MOVEA (for MOVE Address) is used to move data into an address register. In fact the instruction opcode is the same as that used for MOVE, and many assemblers will allow you to simply use MOVE to an address register instead of specifying MOVEA. It is normally a good idea to use MOVEA where required in order to remind yourself that the condition codes are not set.

If we now wanted to set a number of consecutive locations to the same value we could write the following small program to do it.

```
ORG       $1000
MOVEA.L  #$2000,A0      Load start address
MOVE.L   #0,D2          Load value
MOVE.L   D2,(A0)+       Store value and move ...
MOVE.L   D2,(A0)+       .. to next location
MOVE.L   D2,(A0)+       and again
END
```

The first line of the program sets the assembler into absolute mode starting at location $1000. Line two loads address register A0 with a value which will be used as a pointer further on. This pointer is initially $2000. Similarly line three sets all 32 bits of data register D2 to the value 0. Lines four to six take the value stored in register D2 and place it into the location given by the contents of address register A0. The operation is of size long, so the four bytes $2000 to $2003 are set to zero. Because the (A0) is followed by a plus sign, we have asked for the address register to be incremented after the operation has been performed. The address register A0 will be incremented by 4 because the MOVE instruction was of size long. If we had specified MOVE.W then A0 would have been incremented by 2, and if we had used MOVE.B then it would only have been incremented by 1.

The register A0 therefore now contains $2004, and so line five will set bytes $2004 to $2007 to zero, and increment A0 again to $2008. Similarly line six will set bytes $2008 to $200B, leaving A0 containing $200C.

Conditional branches

We have already seen that the MOVE instruction will set the condition codes while moving data from one place to another. We can use this fact to write a small program to clear a large section of memory. Not a very exciting program perhaps, but all we can manage with only two instructions. The new instruction which we require is one found on most computers – the conditional branch.

A conditional branch is an instruction which tests one or more of the condition codes and jumps to another part of the program depending on whether the condition code is set or not. There are several sorts of conditional branch instruction memonics corresponding to the various condition codes. Initially we are only interested in the instructions BEQ and BNE. The former causes the computer to jump to the location specified if the Z status bit is set, otherwise the next instruction after the BEQ is executed. It can be read as 'branch if equal to zero'. Similarly the latter is 'branch if not equal to zero', and causes a jump unless the Z status bit is set.

With these limited tools we can design a program which clears memory from a given location to location zero.

```
        ORG  $1000
        MOVEA.L  #$100,A0     Set up initial pointer
LOOP    MOVE.L  #0,-(A0)      Step pointer down and zero
        MOVE.L  A0,D1        Move pointer into D1
        BNE     LOOP         and loop back until pointer is zero
        END
```

As in the previous example, the first line sets up our program origin, while the next line initialises our pointer register. Line three moves immediate data of zero into the location pointed at by address register A0. The MOVE instruction is of size long, and the address register is used in predecrement mode, so the value in A0 is decremented by 4 **before** the instruction is executed. Thus the first time the instruction is executed A0 will contain $FC, and locations $FC to $FF will be set to zero. Note that the byte at location $100 is not altered.

Line 4 at first seems rather strange, as we are simply moving the value of the pointer into the data register D1. But remember that all MOVE instructions except those where the destination is an address register cause the condition codes to be set. Thus if A0 contained zero then the Z status bit would be set after this operation. The first time through A0 will be $FC, and so the Z bit will not be set. This means that line 5 will cause control to be moved back to line 3, labelled LOOP. Again, A0 will be decremented to $F8 and locations $F8 to $FB will be set to zero. As A0 is still not zero, line 4 will ensure that Z is not set, and we will loop round again. This will continue until A0 is $4. This time when A0 is decremented it will be zero. Locations 0 to 3 will be cleared by line 3, but line 4 will move the value zero from A0 into D1. This will set the Z condition code, so that the branch is not taken, and the program terminates.

Our tiny program could be improved in a number of ways. One way is to replace line 3 by

```
        MOVE.B  #0,-(A0)
```

which would only set the single byte pointed at by A0 to zero. In this case the instruction is of length byte, which means that A0 would be decremented by one before the operation. The program would work in exactly the same way as before, but would only set a single byte each time round the loop rather than four bytes at a time. This will take much longer to execute, as the loop is performed four times as often. The extra time is partly offset by the fact that a MOVE instruction of length byte takes less time than one of length long.

The real difference is that the program would be shorter, as the immediate data will be held as a word rather than as two words within the program. In this case the extra two bytes are a small price to pay for the increase in speed, but as in most computing problems there is always a choice between space and speed.

One way in which the program can be made smaller with no loss of speed is to replace the BNE instruction with

```
BNE.S    LOOP
```

All the conditional branch instructions have a long version and a short version. In either case the value stored with the branch is not the actual location to be jumped to, but a signed number indicating how far away the required label is from the current place in the program. The long version uses two bytes to store this displacement, while the short version only uses one byte. Placing a .S after the memonic tells the assembler to use the short branch version of the instruction. It can only be used when the label to be branched to is less than 128 bytes before or ahead of the branch. The version without a qualifying letter allows branches up to 32767 bytes before or ahead. Some assemblers will use the short form automatically for backwards branches, but if the branch is to a label which has not yet been declared the assembler will always use the long form unless told to do otherwise by specifying the short form.

Comparing data

In the previous section we used the fact that the condition codes are set by the MOVE instruction. This is normally only useful if we want to move a value somewhere, but also check if the value is zero or negative. In many cases we want to compare two values, and this is exactly what the CMP instruction does.

A common use of CMP is to see if two values are the same. If the two operands used in the CMP instruction are identical, then the Z condition code will be set. Thus the section of program

```
CMP.L    D0,D1
BEQ      EQUAL
```

will cause a jump to the label EQUAL if D0 and D1 contain the same value.

The actual operation of CMP is to subtract the first operand from the second and to set the condition codes appropriately. The actual result of the subtraction is thrown away, and the original value of the second operand is unchanged. The condition codes are all either set or cleared except for the X code which is unchanged.

There are four versions of the CMP instruction, and many assemblers will choose the correct version automatically. The CMP form may only be used with a data register as the destination operand. The value compared may be specified as byte, word or long. Any address mode may be used as the source, with one exception. This is when the size is specified as a byte, and in this case the source cannot be held in an address register, although it can be pointed to by one. Thus a valid example would be

```
CMP.B    12(A3),D0
```

which would compare the byte held at offset 12 from the location pointed at by A3 with the low order 8 bits of D0.

The CMPA version of the instruction may only be used with an address register as the destination operand. In this case the value may only be specified as word or long, and any address mode may be used as the source. If the word form of the instruction is used, the value given is sign extended to 32 bits and the resulting long value is used in the comparison. Thus

```
CMPA.W   #$FFFF,A2
```

would set the Z condition code if A2 was equal to -1 ($FFFFFFFF), and would not set Z if A2 contained $FFFF.

The CMPI version may only be used with a data alterable destination, so that the contents of an address register or a program counter relative value may not be used. The source must always be immediate data, and the instruction can be any of the three lengths. Thus

```
CMPI.B   #$0A,-(A0)
```

will decrement the value stored in A0 by 1, and then compare the value $0A with the byte pointed at by the new value of A0. CMPI can be used with a data register as the destination operand, and in this case the operation is the same as if CMP had been used with immediate data as the source operand.

The final version of CMP is used to compare memory locations, and is specified by CMPM. In this case the source and destination operands can only be specified using postincrement address mode. The comparison can take place on a byte, word or long word. This is useful in comparing large sections of memory. Consider the following fragment of program, which will compare 100 bytes of memory starting at location $1000 with 100 bytes starting at $2000.

```
        MOVEA.L #$1000,A0    Load first pointer
        MOVEA.L #$2000,A1    Load second pointer
LOOP    CMPM.B  (A0)+,(A1)+  Do comparison
        BNE.S   NOTSAME      Jump if not equal
        CMPA.L  #$1064,A0    Check end condition
        BNE.S   LOOP         Loop back if more to do
```

Here we load up two address registers with pointers to the area of memory which we wish to compare. Line three compares the two bytes pointed at by the address registers, and increments the pointers. If the two values are not equal then line four jumps out of the loop. If they were equal, we must carry on and check the next two. The address registers have already been incremented ready for the next comparison, but first we must check to see if all the bytes have been examined. Line five compares the first pointer with the base address plus 100. If A0 does not yet equal this value, line six jumps back to label LOOP to look at the next pair of bytes. Otherwise we drop through and we know that the two 100 byte areas are the same.

More conditional branches

So far we have only learnt about conditional branches which test for two types of condition. These are BEQ which branches if the Z bit is set, and BNE which branches if the Z bit is not set. As you would probably suspect, there are are a number of other versions of the Bcc instruction which test other conditions.

The first group of these are governed only by a single bit in the status register. Just as BEQ and BNE cause a branch to be taken depending on the value of the Z bit, BCS and BCC can be used to test the state of the carry bit. The former reads as 'branch if carry set', and branches if the C bit is currently set; the latter is 'branch if carry clear' and jumps if the carry is unset.

BMI and BPL can be used in exactly the same way to test the N bit; 'branch if minus' means that the branch is to be taken if the N bit is set while 'branch if plus' only jumps if the N bit is unset. Note that the N bit is cleared if the value is zero, so that BPL will jump in this case as well.

The final pair in this first group are BVS and BVC which branch if the overflow bit is set or clear.

The second group of conditional branches test a number of conditions before deciding whether to jump. Some of these appear very similar to the simpler tests mentioned earlier, and the only difference is in the treatment of the overflow and carry bits. A number of instructions, such as MOVE, always clear C and V and so in this case the two forms are identical. The difference is only important when handling signed numbers.

BLT and BGE are used when comparing signed numbers, and can be read as 'branch if less than' and 'branch if greater than or equal'. BLT tests the N bit in the same way as BMI, but only branches if the N bit is set and the overflow bit V is unset. If V is set then it will branch if the N bit is also unset. This means that so long as no overflow occurs BLT behaves as BMI; if overflow has happened then BLT behaves like BPL. BGE also tests the N and V bit and jumps if they are both unset or both set. In this respect it behaves like BPL if no overflow has happened and like BMI if it has.

BLS and BHI test the Z and C bit. The first is 'branch if low or same' and will jump if either the carry bit or the zero bit are set. The second is 'branch high' and will only jump if both C and Z are unset. The BCC and BCS are sometimes given the alternative names BHS and BLO, for 'branch if high or same' and 'branch low' respectively.

The most complicated conditional branches are 'branch if less than or equal' and 'branch if greater than'. BLE will jump if the conditions tested in BLT are true but will also jump if the Z bit is set. BGT makes the same test as BGE, but for the branch to take place the Z bit must be unset whether overflow has occurred or not.

We will see later how the same condition names are used in the DBcc and Scc instructions to test the same combinations of status bits. With these instructions the additional conditions T and F are allowed, meaning True and False. The equivalent to BT, or branch if true, is of course spelt BRA. There is no equivalent to BF, which would mean never branch, and this potential combination is taken up by BSR.

A simple memory diagnostic program

We have now learnt sufficient instructions to write a simple memory diagnostic program. We will take an area of memory, and place a certain bit pattern into it. We will then check that the memory has retained the value placed into it. This is a useful check to see if all the RAM chips on a board are behaving themselves. As we have not yet learnt how to perform any input or output, the program will jump to a certain location if it finds any errors. This could be the location of a monitor routine which wrote a message for us — the details are not important here.

```
        ORG     $400
* Define some useful constants
MEMLO   EQU     $1000           lower limit
MEMHI   EQU     $2000           upper limit
TPAT    EQU     $AA             test pattern
MONLOC  EQU     $2000           monitor return address
*
* The memory check program
*
ENTER   MOVEA.L #MEMLO,A0       Set up base pointer
* Fill memory with required value
LP1     MOVE.B  #TPAT,(A0)+     Store value, increment A0
        CMPA.L  #MEMHI,A0       Check limit reached
        BNE.S   LP1             No, keep going
* Check memory has kept that value
        MOVEA.L #MEMLO,A0       Reset base pointer
LP2     CMPI.B  #TPAT,(A0)+     Check value is the same
        BNE     MONLOC          Not the same — error at (A0)-1
        CMPA.L  #MEMHI,A0       Check limit reached
        BNE.S   LP2             No, keep going
* Check complete. Go back and try it again
        BRA.S   ENTER
        END
```

Here the first few lines set up a program origin and define some values using EQU directives. It is always good practice to use EQU to define a name for a particular value, as this makes the program much easier to change later. For example, here our little program tests memory from $1000 to $1FFF. These values are defined by the labels MEMLO and MEMHI. If anyone wanted to change the program to test another area of memory this could easily be done by altering the EQU statements, rather than searching through the program itself trying to find uses of various numbers and altering those.

The program is entered at the label ENTER, where A0 is set to point to the start of the area of memory we wish to test. Label LP1 defines the start of loop, placing the test pattern defined by TPAT into the byte pointed at by A0, and incrementing A0. The next line uses CMPA to check to see if we have filled all the memory required. If not we branch back to LP1, only dropping through when all the memory has been filled.

Once the memory has been filled we reset our pointer A0 and loop through the test region again. If the value stored in memory is not what was expected then we take a branch to MONLOC. Register A0 will already have been incremented and so the actual location in error will be one less than the address held in A0.

Notice the use of MOVEA.L and CMPA.L. In this particular example MOVEA.W and CMPA.W would have done just as well, and would also have made the program shorter. But this would have left a terrible trap for anyone coming along and changing the program later. Consider wishing to extend the upper limit of memory checked from $2000 to $8000. Anyone wishing to do this would look at our program, and think that all that was required was to change the definition of MEMHI from $2000 to $8000. If we had used the word length versions of MOVEA and CMPA then when the test for the end of the loop was made, the processor would take the immediate value defined by MEMHI, sign extend it to 32 bits and then make the comparison with A0. This would cause the loop to terminate only when the value of A0 was $FFFF8000, which is not a valid address. In fact the program would terminate due to a bus error as soon as all the valid memory had been filled. The moral of this example is that it is always sensible to use long versions of instructions when placing addresses into address registers. The other versions should normally only be used when holding data values in address registers.

Comparing and moving zero

There are two special instructions in the repertoire of the 68000 which are used when dealing with the value zero. We have already seen that MOVE can be used with immediate source data to move any value into memory or into a register, and this value could be zero. Similarly the CMP family can be used with immediate data which could also be zero. However an immediate value is represented as one or two extension 16 bit words following the 16 bits of the instruction word, and so the operation

```
MOVE.L  #0,D0
```

will take up 16 bits for the instruction, and 32 bits for the representation of the long value zero. As it is very common to set values to zero, there are two special instructions provided which are only 16 bits long.

The first of these is CLR, which will clear the specified destination to zero. This destination must be data alterable, so that it cannot be used to clear an address register to zero. However a byte, word or long word in memory referenced directly or by an address register may be set to zero. Similarly the low order 8, 16 or 32 bits of a data register may be set to zero.

The condition codes are set as if MOVE had been used to place zero into the destination, so that X is unaffected, Z is set and the others are cleared.

The instruction should be used with care if the memory location is actually part of the I/O page, where memory mapped devices appear as if they are memory locations. The instruction actually reads memory before writing zero into it, which might give strange effects if the action of reading an I/O port affects the associated peripheral.

Similarly, the TST instruction may be used to test whether a value is equal to zero. Again the destination may be specified as any data alterable location, and the size may be byte, word or long. If the value specified is equal to zero then the Z bit will be set, otherwise it will be cleared. Suitable BEQ, BNE or BLE instructions would normally follow.

TST can also be used to see if a value is negative. If it is then the N bit will be set, otherwise it will be cleared. The X bit is not affected and the V and C bits are always cleared. Thus BMI and BPL can be used to test the condition of the N bit. Note that after this instruction BLT will have the same effect as BMI as the carry bit is always clear. Similarly BGT and BPL are also interchangable in this case.

Moving small numbers

Many programmers will wish to use the long form of instructions as much as possible, as the ability to handle 32 bit values is one of the features which makes the 68000 so different from its rivals. However it is a common requirement to initialise registers to zero or a small integer. We have already seen how the CLR instruction may be used to clear a register or memory location to zero, and that this may be used in any of the three sizes.

Initialising a register to a small integer can be done by moving immediate data into the register using the long form of the MOVE instruction. The only problem is that this instruction takes up six bytes; two for the MOVE instruction and four for the immediate data. Obviously all four bytes are required to hold the immediate value if that value is indeed of size long, but it seems rather a pity to waste so much space simply holding bytes which are zero when the immediate value could fit into a byte.

In order to cater for this situation, a special form of the MOVE instruction is provided. The MOVEQ (for Move Quick) instruction is only of size long, and can only be used to move a number which will fit into a byte into a data register. The effect is exactly the same as would be obtained if MOVE was used to move an immediate value in the range −128 to +127 into a data register, except that the MOVEQ instruction only takes up two bytes, with the immediate value packed into the bottom byte of the instruction. The entire data register is altered, with the data sign extended if required. The N or Z status bits are set if the value so moved is negative or zero, while the V and C bits are always cleared and X is unchanged.

The MOVEQ instruction takes less time to execute than the long form of the CLR instruction acting on a data register, and so is a better way of clearing an entire data register to zero. Remember that MOVEQ is always of size long, and can only be used on data registers.

Testing bits

There are a number of instructions which can be used on a single bit. These will be described in detail in chapter 6, but one of them is of interest here. This is the BTST instruction, which is used to test a particular bit in the destination. If the bit is equal to zero, then the Z bit is set. If it is one, then the Z bit is unset; all other condition codes are unchanged.

The destination location is not affected, and may be specified using any data addressing mode. The action of the instruction varies depending on whether the destination is a memory location or a data register. In the former case, a byte is read from memory and a bit in that byte is tested. The low order bit is specified as bit 0, and the high order bit as 7. Numbers larger than 7 are regarded as modulo 8.

If a data register is used as the destination, then bit numbers range from 0 to 31, hence allowing all the bits in the register to be tested. Again, if the number is larger than 31 it is regarded as modulo 32. The size of the BTST instruction therefore varies between byte and long depending on the destination operand, and is not specified by the programmer.

The bit number is given as the source operand, and may be specified in two ways. The first is to use an immediate form; in this case the value given is used as the bit number. The alternative is to give a data register, which will cause the processor to use the number held in the data register as the bit number. In either case the bit number is used modulo 8 or 32 depending on whether the destination is memory or a data register.

It is important to remember that the bit number itself is used, not the bit pattern representing the particular bit to be tested.

Testing conditions

We have already seen how the Bcc family of instructions can be used to branch depending on the state of various combinations of the condition codes. This is the most common use of the condition codes, but there are two other instructions which inspect the condition code value. The first of these is Scc, or Set according to condition code. This tests the value of one or more of the condition codes, using the same set of conditions as the Bcc family. If the condition is satisfied, then the byte defined as the destination is set to $FF. If the condition is not satisfied, then the destination byte is set to zero. Thus, for example,

```
        Scc     BYTELOC       Set BYTELOC according to condition
```

provides in a single instruction the equivalent of the following.

```
        Bcc     NXT           Branch if condition satisfied
        CLR.B   BYTELOC       Clear BYTLOC, not satisfied
        BRA.S   NXT1          Branch to end
NXT     MOVE.B  #$FF,BYTELOC  Set BYTELOC to $FF
NXT1    ....    Rest of program
```

Notice that Scc can only be used to set single bytes, which must be specified using data alterable addressing modes. It is also a useful way of always setting a byte to $FF, because using the condition test TRUE

```
        ST      BYTELOC
```

will unconditionally set all the bits in BYTELOC. The equivalent test using FALSE (SF) is identical to using the byte form of the CLR instruction.

The Scc instruction is normally useful for remembering the state of a particular condition code for testing at a later date.

Loop control

One of the most common operations performed in a computer is that of performing a set of instructions over and over again. This loop is normally controlled by an iteration variable, which is incremented until it reaches a certain value.

The 68000 provides an instruction to help with controlling loops, but it works in the opposite direction to that which is usually required. That is, it **decrements** an iteration variable. It is also slightly confusing because the iteration stops when the variable has become negative, not when it becomes zero.

The family of instructions are known as DBcc, read as 'Decrement and Branch'. In fact the full operation of the instruction is to first test a condition code, and to move onto the decrement and branch part only if the condition is not satisfied. We will first look at the use of the instruction when the condition is never satisfied, i.e. DBF or decrement and branch with condition false. This is the most common version used, and most assemblers allow the alternative syntax DBRA.

DBRA takes a data register as the source operand, and a label as the destination operand. The instruction is always of size word. If the value of the register is zero, then the next instruction is executed. Otherwise the value in the register is decremented by one and a jump is made to the label given as the destination.

The previous description is not quite correct, as in fact the decrement always takes place on the register, and so the register used will not be zero when the loop has completed. Also only the low order 16 bits of the register are used as the counter. The label may be before or after the DBRA instruction, although it is usually before it. Consider the following program fragment.

```
        MOVE.L  #$2000,A1       Set up pointer
        MOVE.W  #19,D0          Set up counter
LOOP    CLR.B   (A1)+           Clear byte and increment pointer
        DBRA    D0,LOOP         Loop while D0 >= 0
```

Here the low order 16 bits of D0 are used as a counter. Initially these are set to 19, while an address register A1 is set up to point to a memory location. At the label LOOP the byte referenced by A1 is cleared to zero and A1 is incremented by 1, as the CLR was of size byte. The DBRA instruction decrements D0, and checks to see if the result is negative. If not, control is passed back to LOOP. This happens until D0 is zero, when the decrement performed as part of DBRA gives a negative value. In this case the jump to LOOP is not made, and we exit the program with the low order 16 bits of D0 set to $FFFF and A1 set to $2014.

In many cases a loop is to be executed a variable number of times, and if the iteration count is initially zero then the loop is not to be executed at all. In this case the DBRA instruction should be placed at the end of the loop, and the instructions just before the start of the loop should set up the iteration count into a suitable register, and make an unconditional branch to the DBRA instruction at the end of the loop. Note that the iteration count, and not one less than the count, should be placed in the register. If the iteration count was zero to start with no branch will occur at the DBRA and so the loop will be entirely bypassed.

The DBRA version of the DBcc instruction is normally the most useful, but the full form is extremely powerful. Here a condition is specified, and if the condition is true then the DBcc instruction has no effect. Normal execution continues with the instruction immediately following. If the condition is not met, then the data register is decremented and the branch specified is taken only if the result is not equal to −1.

This allows for a number of extremely powerful looping constructs. For example, a program may be required to copy data from one place to another until a byte equal to some value is found. The destination area may only be of a limited length, and so the copy operation is also to stop if the destination has been filled. Such situations may occur when reading a line of information from the terminal into an internal buffer. The copy is to terminate if the character 'return' is found, but is also to stop if a line longer than that allowed for is entered. We might use the following program segment.

```
CR       EQU      $0D            ASCII carriage return
         MOVEA.L  #$2000,A3      Set up pointer to buffer
         MOVE.W   #79,D0         Allow for 80 characters
RCH      ...      read character into D1
         MOVE.B   D1,(A3)+       Save character
         CMP.B    #CR,D1         Check to see if end of line
         DBEQ     D0,RCH         Loop unless return or buffer full
```

The first two lines initialise A3 as a pointer into the buffer and D0 as the size of that buffer in bytes. In each iteration of the loop we read a character from the console in some way, and save it in the buffer using postincrement addressing mode. Finally we compare the character read in with the ASCII code for carriage return. If the character read in was indeed a return, the DBEQ instruction has no effect and the loop has terminated. If the end of the input line has not been reached we branch back and read another character only if there will be room in the buffer.

Simple input and output

All the previous examples have assumed that the test programs were running under a monitor, which would allow you to enter your program and to start it running. Normally such monitors also provide a mechanism for writing information to a terminal connected to the computer, and also to accept information from the terminal.

Alternatively you may be running your programs under an operating system, in which case this will provide some mechanism to input and output information. In either case it is likely that the method used to communicate with the outside world will be a connection to a serial line, onto which a terminal of some sort can be connected. The most common way for this serial line connection to be provided is by the use of a special chip, known as an ACIA or Asynchronous Communication Interface Adapter. This description applies to the 6850 ACIA, but most input and output chips work in a similar fashion. We will not go into too much detail about this device; it simply handles all the work required to send and receive a byte of information down a serial line.

An ACIA appears in part of the memory space of a 68000. Each ACIA has two ports, a control port and a data port. In an 8 bit computer, these ports are in adjacent memory locations. On the 68000, they appear as the low order bytes of two adjacent 16 bit words.

Initially the ACIA must be reset – this is done by writing the value 3 to the control port. The instruction manual for the ACIA tells us that we should wait a little while after resetting it to give it time to settle down.

We must next select the characteristics of the serial line, such as the parity, whether interrupts are to be enabled and so on. Initially we will use the ACIA in polled mode – this means that unless the 68000 is checking the port for characters arriving it is possible that characters may be missed. The ACIA is clever enough to tell us that we have missed a character, but there is nothing we can do to find out what it was we missed. Later on we will see how to run an ACIA in interrupt mode, but for now polled mode will do. We will use the value $15 as the setup mode for the ACIA, which should just be regarded as a magic value. If you actually need to set up an ACIA you should read the standard documentation about it to find out what the values mean. This magic value is written into the control port.

Once an ACIA is set up, the low order two bits of the control port are used to tell us about the state of the data port. Bit number 0 goes to a one if a character has arrived down the serial line. We can then read the character from the data port, which turns bit 0 off until the next character arrives. Bit number 1 is used to tell us if the ACIA is happy to send a character down the line. If it is one, then we can write a byte into the data port and this will be sent down the line. This takes a little time, and while the ACIA is busy doing this bit 1 is set to a zero. Once the byte has been transmitted bit 1 is set to one again, and we can send another character. The sending and receiving of characters is entirely separate – hence the Asynchronous part of the title.

All of this might sound a little complicated, but in fact an ACIA is very easy to use, especially now we have learnt some more of the 68000 instruction set. Let us try to write the text "Hello!" to the terminal.

```
* Values required by ACIA
A_RST    EQU     $03             RESET code
A_INIT   EQU     $15             Magic setup value
A_RDY    EQU     1               Bit set when ready
A_CTRL   EQU     $840021         Control port memory location
A_DATA   EQU     $840023         Data port memory location
*
         ORG     $1000
* Initialise ACIA
ENTER    MOVE.B  #A_RST,A_CTRL Reset ACIA
         MOVE.W  #1000,D0        Initialise counter
WAIT     DBRA    D0,WAIT         Waste time looping back
         MOVE.B  #A_INIT,A_CTRL Set up ACIA
* Send string down the serial line
         MOVEA.L #STRING,A0      Pointer to string
NXT      BTST    #A_RDY,A_CTRL Test ok to transmit
         BEQ.S   NXT             Not ready yet, try again
         MOVE.B  (A0)+,A_DATA Write byte into data port
         TST.B   (A0)            See if next byte is zero
         BNE.S   NXT             No, loop back to write it
* Data location for string
STRING   DC.B    'Hello!'        Message
         DC.B    0               Marker at end of string
```

The first few lines define some useful names for us, including the reset and intialisation codes for the ACIA, and the location of the control and data ports in the memory map. We start the program at the label ENTER, which places the reset value into the control port. We must now waste some time, so we initialise D0 as a counter and immediately decrement it using the DBRA instruction. The processor will jump back to the start of the same instruction until D0 becomes negative, or until we have executed the DBRA 1001 times. Finally we write the magic value associated with initialisation into the control port, and we are ready to write out the string.

The instruction immediately before the label NXT moves the immediate value of the label STRING into register A0. If we look at the end of the program, we can see the label is defined as referring to some memory which we have initialised to the characters in our string. Thus A0 now points to the very first character of the string. It is also worth noticing here that there is a byte containing zero immediately after the string, which we shall use to indicate the end of the message.

The label NXT refers to a BTST instruction. If bit 1 of the control port is zero then the ACIA is not yet ready for another character. In this case the Z bit is set in the condition code, and the conditional branch on the next line will cause us to go back and check the bit again. We will sit in this loop until bit 1 of the ACIA control port becomes set, when it is possible for us to send a character. This is done by using A0 in postincrement mode, thus moving the character from the string into the output port and incrementing the pointer all in one go.

Finally we have to see if we have finished yet. The TST instruction uses address register A0 again, but does not alter its value. If A0 now points to a byte which is zero, then we have finished writing out string. The Z condition code will be set, and we drop through the BNE instruction following the TST. If not we loop back to NXT and write out the next character, waiting for the ACIA to become ready first of all.

Notice that is normally better to test that the ACIA is ready before we intend to use it, and not to wait after we have used it until it is ready again. The internal logic of the ACIA works independently of the 68000 processor, so we might as well get on with some useful work while the output is taking place.

Note that once the string has been written out the processor will attempt to execute the instruction following the BNE. As we have written it, this is whatever instruction is specified by the string "Hello!", which is probably garbage. Normally an instruction to return to the monitor would be placed at the end – the actual details are unimportant.

Moving data to peripherals

You have seen in the previous section how the ACIA had two ports, and how they appeared as the low order bytes of two adjacent memory words. The specification of an ACIA will normally show the ports as appearing in consecutive bytes of memory, but the ACIA was originally designed for 8 bit microprocessors. If an ACIA is connected in an 8 bit machine then the two ports are next door to each other in the memory map, but in the 68000 they appear in alternate bytes. This is true of any peripheral device connected to a 68000 when it was originally intended for an 8 bit machine, and is due to the 16 bit data lines generated by the 68000.

In many cases it is perfectly simple to allow for this, and to read or write from the required bytes in memory. However in some circumstances this can be inconvenient or slow, and so a special version of MOVE is provided which attempts to deal with the problem. MOVEP (for Move Peripheral) takes a data register and a location specified by an address register and displacement. When the data register is the source, the contents held in it is placed a byte at a time into alternate memory locations, starting at the one specified by the address register and displacement. MOVEP is only available in word or long forms. Consider the following example.

```
MOVE.L   #$01020304,D1 Load data
MOVEA.L  #$C00000,A1   Load address register
MOVEP.L  D1,1(A1)      Move data
```

Here we load D1 with the value $01020304, and set A1 to the address $C00000. It is asssumed that four peripheral control ports are mapped to locations $C00001, $C00003, $C00005 and $C00007. The MOVEP instruction takes the high order byte and places this in the location specified, which is $C00001. It then takes the next byte from the register, which is $02 in our example, and places it into the next memory location plus one, or $C00003. The next byte goes to the next odd location, while the least significant byte is placed in location $C00007.

If the data register is the destination then the operation is reversed, and alternate bytes from memory are placed into the register. MOVEP should be used with care, as it is very different from MOVE in some respects. Firstly the condition codes are not affected, while if MOVE to a data register is used they are altered. Secondly only alternate bytes of memory take part in the transfer, and these may be odd or even bytes depending on whether the start address is odd or even. There is nothing special about the way in which the bytes are accessed, and in many cases a byte sized MOVE is simpler. However in those cases where a large amount of information is to be transferred the instruction is useful. One circumstance might be when a floating point processor intended for 8 bit machines is attached to a 68000. A full 32 bit value could be transferred to the other processor in one simple MOVEP operation, while the alternative would be four byte sized MOVEs and three shift instructions.

Chapter 4

Stacks and subroutines

One of the most common ways of organising the data used in a program inside any computer is by the use of stacks. This technique places each new data item which we want to remember 'on top of' the last one, much like placing one piece of paper on top of another. When we wish to remove a data item, we must extract the one which we placed most recently on the stack. We can then remove the previous item or add a new one.

The stack is represented in the computer by an area of memory which we use from high locations to low locations. Because of this 'upside down' nature of the representation, we often talk about the 'top of stack' - meaning the lowest memory location currently in use.

Initially a register is set up to point to the highest location in the stack area. When we need to remember a value, we decrement the pointer by the size of the object we wish to store, and place the object at the memory pointed at by the updated register. If we need to remember another value, we do the same operation, updating the pointer (the stack pointer) and placing the object adjacent to the first one we stored.

The only problem with a stack is that we can only take objects off the stack in the opposite order in which they were stored. So we can remove the second object on the stack by reversing the process, reading the information out of the location pointed at by the stack pointer and adding the size of the object to the pointer. We can now place a new object on the stack or remove the first one we placed there.

The 68000 provides us with eight address registers, all of which can be used as stack pointers. The predecrement and postincrement modes can be used, so that all that is needed is to set up a register with a suitable initial 'top of stack' pointer. We can then use this area of memory to save results in, and this is particularly useful if we need to use some registers in a calculation, but do not want to destroy the original contents of the registers. For example,

```
        MOVEA.L  #$2000,A3     Set up A3 to stack top
* Set up data registers to important values
        ...
        MOVE.L   D0,-(A3)      Save register D0 on stack
        MOVE.L   D1,-(A3)      Save register D1 on stack
        MOVE.L   #$123,D0      Use D0 and D1 in some way
        ...
        MOVE.L   (A3)+,D1      Restore register D1
        MOVE.L   (A3)+,D0      Restore D0
        ...                    Use old values of D0 and D1
```

In this example we set up A3 as a stack pointer, and then go on to load some useful values in all the data registers. In a later section of the program we still need all the values in the data registers, but we have run out of registers needed in another calculation.

One possible solution would be to store the previous values of D0 and D1 in some named memory location, and to retrieve them once we have finished. But there might be several places where we need to do this. Using a stack is easier in this case. More importantly, by using a stack we can ensure that we write both pure code and position independent code. The advantages of this were described in earlier chapters.

We therefore save the current values of the data registers on the stack. Initially A3 contains $2000. As we are using a long MOVE operation, the predecrement addressing mode means that 4 is subtracted from A3. The contents of D0 is then saved in the location pointed to by the new value of A3 – in other words it is stored in bytes $1FFC to $1FFF. The next instruction saves the contents of D1 in bytes $1FF8 to $1FFB, and A3 ends up containing $1FF8.

We are now free to use D1 and D2 in some calculation. When we have finished we restore the old values by loading from the location pointed at by A3 using the postincrement addressing mode. Thus the previous value of D1 is loaded from location $1FF8, and D0 is loaded from $1FFC. It is important to remember to load the values back off the stack in the opposite order to that in which they were stored.

There is a special form of the MOVE instruction which is especially useful when dealing with stacks. The example above saved the value of two of the registers on the stack, and used two instructions to do so. If we had wanted to save the values of all sixteen registers we would have had to use sixteen instructions, which would have used up 32 bytes of code and taken a considerable time to execute.

The MOVEM instruction is designed to help with saving values on a stack. It specifies that between one and sixteen of the registers are to be saved on a stack or loaded from one. The instruction takes a list of registers as one argument and an effective address as the other. The list of registers is converted into a word value, where a bit set to one indicates that the respective register is to take part in the move operation. This form means that the entire sixteen registers can be moved to or from a stack using an instruction only four bytes long, and in a much shorter time than using sixteen separate instructions.

Our example could be modified so that it read as follows.

```
        MOVEA.L  #$2000,A3     Set up A3 to stack top
* Set up data registers to important values
        . . .
        MOVEM.L  D0-D1,-(A3)   Save registers D0 and D1 on stack
        MOVE.L   #$123,D0      Use D0 and D1 in some way
        . . .
        MOVEM.L  (A3)+,D0-D1   Restore registers D0 and D1
        . . .                  Use old values of D0 and D1
```

The MOVEM instruction takes a list of registers in the form of the first register, a hyphen and the last register. All registers between the first and last inclusive are transferred to or from the stack. Another form for the register list is a register name, a slash and another register name. The two possibilities can be mixed, so for example

```
        MOVEM.L  D1-D4/D7/A0-A2/A6,-(A3)
```

will save registers D1 to D4 inclusive, D7, A0 to A2 and A6. Some assemblers will not accept a mixture of data registers and address registers in a range, so that the form

```
        MOVEM.L  D0-D7/A0-A6,-(A7)
```

would be required to save all the registers except A7 onto the stack pointed at by A7.

The order in which the registers are saved on the stack is independent of the order in which the list is specified to the assembler, as the assembler simply sets the relevant bits in the instruction to indicate that the named registers are to take part in the transfer. The order in which registers are saved is from A7 to A0 and then D7 to D0; they are restored in the opposite order so that D0 is loaded first if it is specified in the register list, then D1 and so on up to A0 and finally A7.

In the examples given so far, we have always used the predecrement address mode for saving values and the postincrement mode for restoring them again. When this mode is used the registers are transferred as indicated, and the address register used as the stack pointer is incremented or decremented by the total size of the registers transferred. In this way the MOVEM instruction behaves very much like the equivalent number of MOVE instructions required to save or restore the registers. However there are a number of differences.

Firstly, there are only Word or Long versions of MOVEM – it is not possible to save single byte values on a stack using this operation. If Word values are restored then the entire value of the register is reloaded with the 32 bit value obtained by sign extending the word read from the stack. This means that it is not possible to save the bottom sixteen bits of some registers, use the bottom half of them in a calculation and then restore them without losing the top sixteen bits of their value. It is therefore normally only sensible to use the long form of the MOVEM instruction and save the entire contents of all the registers.

Secondly, the MOVEM instruction uses what is technically called 'pre-fetch'. All this means is that the 68000 processor tries to transfer the registers as quickly as possible, and in order to do this it reads the memory locations it is going to need a short time before it actually requires them. This speeds up the multiple transfer, but when the processor gets to the end of the list of registers it has read one word of memory too much. Normally this is not important, as the final content of the stack pointer is correct, and it does not matter if one word of memory is read and then forgotten. The only time it does matter is when the stack starts at the highest available location in memory. In this case the registers will be stored in locations running down from the top of memory, but when they are restored the processor will attempt to read the word just beyond the top of memory. It is going to forget the value obtained in this way, but the access will normally cause a bus error and the program will not work as expected.

Finally the MOVE instruction will alter the condition codes while MOVEM does not. This enables a condition code to be set in a subroutine to indicate whether it worked or not, and this code will remain unchanged as the original values of the registers are restored.

Earlier we remarked that the registers are transferred in the form stated only if using the predecrement or postincrement address modes. The MOVEM instruction may be used with other address modes which are control modes. If the transfer is taking place to memory then the address mode must be control alterable – in other words the program counter relative mode can only be used when reading from memory.

When used with an address mode other than predecrement or postincrement the order of transfer is always the same. This order is D0 to D7 and then A0 to A7, just as if the postincrement address mode was used. Thus

        MOVEM.L D0–D7,$2000

would store the contents of D0 in bytes $2000 to $2003, D1 in $2004 to $2007 and so on. To reload them again

        MOVEM.L $2000,D0–D7

would be needed.

Subroutines

In one of the earlier MOVEM examples we used A7 as the address register holding the stack pointer. Although any address register can be used in the predecrement or postincrement mode as a stack pointer, it is normal to use A7. This is because of the action of a number of other instructions which assume that A7 is pointing to an area of memory which can be used as a stack. In fact there are two separate versions of register A7, called the user stack pointer or USP, and the supervisor stack pointer or SSP. For now we can assume that A7 always refers to the supervisor stack pointer.

When writing a program for the 68000 it is normal practice to ensure that the stack pointer is set up to the top of a stack area before starting any real work. This will often be done by the operating system or monitor which is providing the facilities for running the program, but it can always be done explicitly by, for example,

```
MOVEA.L $2000,A7
```

which will set up the area below $2000 as a stack. Chaos can ensue if the stack area is overwritten, so it is normally wise to leave a more than generous margin for the stack to grow - we will see in a minute how this can happen. So we will allow our stack to grow from location $2000 down to $1000, and this means that we can start our program at location $2000 upwards. Remember from the discussion of MOVEM that the byte pointed at by the initial value of the stack pointer is not actually written to as we use the predecrement addressing mode which alters the stack pointer before using it.

Once we have set up our stack pointer we can start to use instructions which assume that A7 is indeed set to a valid stack area. Perhaps the most obvious is the Branch to Subroutine instruction, or BSR. This is a very important instruction which allows a jump to be made to another area of program in the same way as BRA; in fact in many ways it is identical except that when you use BRA to jump somewhere you have no way of finding out how you arrived at your destinaton.

There might be several places where the instruction

```
BRA ERROR
```

occurs in a program. At the label ERROR you may wish to give some error message and stop. There is no way for the code at ERROR to find out the place where the branch was made. We could place a value in a register or a fixed location in memory to signify the reason we made the jump to ERROR, so that a suitable message was printed out. We might want to write out this message and then continue with the normal execution of the program. In this case we would use the BSR instruction instead. The action of the processor is to first of all save the address of the next instruction, and then make the branch to the label ERROR. The code at ERROR can then use this saved address to return to when it has finished, so that once it has written the message out execution can continue at the instruction immediately following the BSR. It could also inspect this saved address and use it to say exactly where the error occurred.

The value saved by BSR is called the **return address**, and you have probably guessed by now that it is saved on the stack pointed at by A7. If you could get hold of the address of the next instruction, say in a register called PC, then the action of BSR would be similar to

```
MOVE.L  PC,-(A7)     Save return address on stack
BRA     ERROR        Branch to subroutine
```

In fact there is no way of explictly referencing the value of the program counter; the BSR instruction decrements A7, stores the return address at the four bytes referenced by this new value and then branches to the label all in one go.

We now want to be able to get hold of this value saved on the stack and jump back to the instruction after the BSR. The value can be read explicitly from the top of the stack if required, so that we could return by using code something like

```
        MOVEA.L (A7)+,A6        Extract return address
        JMP     (A6)           And jump to that location
```

The normal way of returning is by using RTS or Return from Subroutine. This is exactly the inverse of BSR, and it reads the return address from the value saved on the stack, increments A7 by four so that the stack slot is now available once again, and then jumps to this new address.

The advantage of using a stack is now clear, as we can use BSR as many times as we like, even within sections of code which have themselves been entered via another BSR. Each time the value of A7 is decremented by four and the new return address saved in the next slot on the stack. Each time an RTS is encountered the stack is incremented and execution continues at the instruction just after the BSR which was used to enter the subroutine.

It is important to remember the special use of A7, and to make sure that it always points to a suitable stack area. Some assemblers provide the synonym of SP (for Stack Pointer) for register A7, and using this reminds you that it is not a normal address register. It can, of course, be used in many circumstances just like any other address register, but there is one important difference. The values stored on the stack must be aligned to an even address, and the hardware ensures, that this is so. This means that if you use a byte sized instruction specifying register A7 in predecrement or postincrement mode, the value of A7 will be altered by two, not one as would happen with any of the other registers.

The idea of a subroutine is a very important one, and anyone with any experience of programming will have met it before. The idea is that instead of writing a section of code many times in order to perform some operation, we write it once and use it as a subroutine. The most obvious example might be the code required to write out a character, such as described in chapter 3. It would be very wasteful of program space if each time we wanted to write a character we had to include the code to test to see if an ACIA was ready before placing the character into the output port. Instead we write a subroutine to do this, and then use BSR to call the subroutine to write the character. When the character has been written an RTS will drop us back to whatever we were doing before.

```
WRCH    BTST    #1,A_CTRL
        BEQ.S   WRCH
        MOVE.B  DO,A_DATA
        RTS
```

This subroutine will write a character to a device connected to a serial port, assuming that it has previously been correctly set up. To use it, all we need to do is to include a BSR to the label WRCH, having first placed the character to be written in the bottom byte of register D0. The subroutine then tests to see if the ACIA is busy — if so it loops round again until it is ready. Then the character passed in D0 is placed into the data register, and control is passed back to the instruction following the BSR which brought us here.

Normally a programmer will have a stock of ready to use subroutines available 'off the shelf'. Nearly all programs have some area of similarity – for example nearly all programs are going to want to write out results of some sort. It is therefore normal to divide a program up into subroutines as much as possible, so that the useful parts can be saved and included later in another program. A normal subroutine library will have very many different subroutines in it. There are a great number of useful operations which may be required when simply performing output, besides simply writing out a character. For example, we might want to write out a string, or a number in decimal or hexadecimal, and so on.

This subroutine library can be built up a little at a time, but there are a number of good programming practices which should be followed. These are good habits to get into no matter what language or what processor you use, but we are fortunate in that the 68000 instruction set helps us write well structured programs.

The first good practice is to ensure that all subroutines are usable under all circumstances. For example, let us consider extending our subroutine library to include a subroutine to write out a string. We will call it using BSR with address register A4 pointing to a string. We will define a string as being a sequence of characters terminated by a byte containing zero. We might write the following.

```
WRITES  MOVE.B   (A4)+,D0     Load byte from string
        BEQ.S    WOVER        Branch if end of string
        BSR.S    WRCH         Write out character
        BRA.S    WRITES       Back to next character
WOVER   RTS
```

Here we extract a byte from the string and increment A4 ready for next time. If the byte is zero then we branch to the label WOVER and return to whoever called us. Otherwise we use another subroutine in our library to write out the character, and loop back to get the next byte from the string. Notice the use of the short form of the Branch to Subroutine instruction specified as BSR.S. This is just like BRA.S, and is simply a shorter version of the instruction which can be used when the label is less than 128 bytes away.

Although this may serve our needs perfectly well, there are a number of problems with this routine. The first fault is that if we use the subroutine WRITES we must remember that D0 is corrupted – in fact the bottom byte will always be set to zero. In our immediate application we may not care what happens to register D0, but if we want to make this a useful subroutine which can be used in all cases then it is extremely bad practice to corrupt a register.

Looking at the code more carefully, we can also see that the address register A4 is corrupted. This is set to point to the byte just beyond the end of the string. Although the user of the subroutine must know that his string is to be passed in A4, it is not really fair of us to alter the value of A4 as a side effect of writing the string out for him. A general useful rule is that subroutines should not alter registers, except of course when a result from the subroutine is being passed back in a register.

Having decided that it is bad programming style to alter registers, we must decide where to save the old values of registers which we are going to use. One possibility is to simply allocate an area of memory and use that as storage. Although this will appear to work, there are a number of problems. Firstly we would have to use a different area of storage for each subroutine, otherwise one subroutine could not call another without the possibility of having the saved values overwritten by another subroutine attempting to save register contents. This would be wasteful of space and difficult to organise. Secondly we would have to make sure that we did not use the storage area allocated to each subroutine for some other purpose in the main program which we were attempting to write. Thirdly the program would not be re-entrant, the full details of which were described in chapter 2.

The answer is of course to save register values on the user stack, using MOVEM where approriate. We have already allocated a register to point to an area of memory in order for us to use BSR. As long as the area is big enough for all the saved registers and the return addresses in the maximum nesting of subroutines then we shall be fine. The advantage is that this is an efficient use of space, as we only use space when it is actually required. We might have several hundred subroutines all wanting to save registers, but the maximum stack use would only be that corresponding to the highest number of subroutines called from each other.

We can now write our improved subroutine to print out a string

```
WRITES   MOVEM.L  D0/A4,-(SP)   Save registers
WR1      MOVE.B   (A4)+,D0      Extract byte
         BEQ.S    WR2           Branch if end
         BSR.S    WRCH          Write character
         BRA.S    WR1           Get next character
WR2      MOVEM.L  (SP)+,D0/A4   Restore registers
         RTS
```

Now we can use WRITES from wherever we like, confident that none of the registers will be altered. In fact, no memory location will be altered except beyond the end of the current stack pointer, and this is an area which is known to be liable to be altered as a result of subroutine calls anyway.

There are two other rules which should be borne in mind when writing general purpose subroutines. The first is that a consistent set of registers should be used for arguments passed over to subroutines and results returned from them. Thus one might always expect arguments in registers D1, D2, etc., and a single result returned in D0. Clearly this is not always possible, as some routines will expect arguments in data registers and some in address registers, but it is useful as a general rule; the programmer is less likely to become confused about what value must be placed in which register before a particular subroutine is called.

Finally it is important to ensure that there is normally only one exit point from a subroutine. Rather than have several RTS instructions in a subroutine it is better practice to have one and branch to that location from other places as required. This means that restoring the registers, deallocating the stack and so on can be done all in one place. Then if the subroutine has to be altered to use, and hence save, an extra register, we need only change the code at the single entry and exit points. It is a very common programming error to save a register on the stack and then accidentally forget to restore it before executing the RTS. The effect is catastrophic as the program jumps to the location specified by the value of the register saved on the stack, which might refer to anywhere. This is a particularly difficult error to locate, as the debugging information will refer to the new program counter, while what is required is information about why the program was there in the first place.

Absolute jumps

It is clearly important to be able to jump to another part of a program, and we have already seen the use of instructions such as BRA which enable us to set up loops. We have also looked at BSR which allows us to call subroutines, and conditional branches such as BEQ.

In all these cases the instruction has been called a branch rather than a jump, and there is a good reason for this. All these branch instructions specify that program control is to be transferred to an address relative to our current position. Although we may write a statement such as

        BRA   LOOP

the assembler converts this to an instruction which contains the difference between the current value of the program counter and the address of the label LOOP. This address offset can be negative or positive, depending on whether we want to jump backwards or forwards. The offset can be specified as a word, so that we use sixteen bits to hold the offset, or as a byte if we use the short form of the instruction.

The alternative to using BRA is JMP, which represents an absolute jump. The address given as part of the JMP instruction is an actual address, and control is transferred to it when the instruction is executed. The effect of

        JMP   LOOP

will be the similar to the BRA instruction, but with a number of differences.

Firstly the JMP instruction will be longer when jumping to a label, as the full address is given in the instruction.

Secondly a section of code using JMP to jump to a label within itself may not be position independent. The 68000 contains a number of instructions which allow code to be written no matter where it loaded in memory. For example, a BRA instruction may specify that a jump to the address 24 bytes away from the current position. This will work no matter where the program is placed in memory. If a program uses the JMP instruction then the value may be specified using any control addressing mode. If the address was specified as an absolute value then it would refer to a single, specific memory location. The program would only work if it was loaded into memory at the address specified by the ORG statement at the start.

In many cases it is perfectly acceptable to load a program into memory at a given address, but it may not be possible if the machine is running an operating system. Here a program may well be loaded into any available space, and if it is position independent then it will run without alteration. Otherwise the program will have to contain some relocation information. This is information generated by some assemblers which allows the operating system to alter those addresses held as part of instructions. This ensures that the program will work at the address at which it is loaded. Unfortunately not all assemblers produce suitable relocation information, so is good practice to write position independent code.

Another advantage of assembly code which is position independent is that it means that a program can not only be loaded anywhere in memory, it can also be moved around if required. Unless great care is taken this code shuffling cannot happen while the program is running, as the stack may contain return addresses which refer to absolute locations in memory. But it can certainly be done between runs of the program.

The JMP instruction can be used in position independent programs to great effect – it is only position dependent when used to jump to a label in your own section of code. A common use for it is to jump to program sections which are known to reside at certain memory locations. For example a monitor may live in EPROM at a known location, and contain a warmstart entry address which should be entered when your own program has finished. We would then end our program with

        JMP   WARMS

which would ensure that we entered the monitor no matter where our program was loaded.

The BSR instruction also has a counterpart, called JSR. Again, JSR takes an address rather than an offset, and could be used to call subroutines known to exist in specific memory locations.

The JMP and JSR instructions are very important, mainly because they take any control addressing mode as the address. In our examples above we have used the absolute addressing mode to enable us to jump to a known memory location. We could also use the program counter relative mode to reference locations in our program, while still maintaining position independence. In this case the effect would be very similar to using BRA or BSR.

Perhaps the most useful addressing mode available here is one of the indexed modes. Consider writing a program which worked off single letter commands. For each command typed at the terminal, a subroutine is called to perform that job. We can program this by creating a table which contains four bytes for each of the ASCII characters. Each entry in the table represents the address of a routine which must be called if that character is typed. Thus the first entry in the table will be the routine to be called if a zero byte is typed, which corresponds to the ASCII character NUL. The routine to be called if 'A' is typed is placed at the offset for the character 'A', which is long word offset $41.

```
ASL.L    #2,D0          Multiply by four
MOVEA.L  #TABLE,A3      Get table address
JSR      0(A3,D0.W)     Call subroutine to do job
```

The first line shifts the contents of register D0 to the left by two places, thus multiplying it by 4. This is required because each slot in the table will take up four bytes. The second line takes the address of the table and loads it into address register A3. Finally the last line extracts the address stored at the location pointed at by the sum of A3 and D0, and calls it as a subroutine, placing a suitable return address on the stack.

Effective addresses

The last example used the MOVEA instruction with an immediate addressing mode to load the value of TABLE into A3. Although this works perfectly well, the instruction is not position independent. What we are actually doing is asking the 68000 to load a data value into a register. This data item happens to be the value of a label declared at the start of a table. If the program is not loaded into memory at the position declared by the ORG statement then the MOVEA instruction will still load this data value, even though it does not now refer to the start of our table.

The solution is to use the LEA instruction, which stands for Load Effective Address. The instruction can only be used with an address register as the destination, and it causes the address given as the source to be evaluated in the same way as if the instruction was MOVE, for instance. Instead of then loading the value at the address, the address itself is placed in the destination register.

Consider the following program segment.

```
     ORG     $1000
LAB  DC.L    1234
     MOVEA.L LAB,A3
     MOVEA.L #LAB,A3
     LEA.L   LAB,A3
```

Here we declare four bytes of memory at address $1000, initialised to 1234. The first MOVEA instruction will evaluate the address given by LAB, which is $1000, and then proceed to load the contents of that location, which is 1234. The second MOVEA will load register A3 with the immediate value given by the label LAB, which is $1000. However this instruction is position dependent, and will only work if the program is assembled in absolute mode.

A much better may to perform this operation is to load the address using LEA. This evaluates the address given by the label LAB using program counter relative addressing if required, thus making the code position independent. Remember that LEA evaluates the address, and places the address itself into the specified register. It does not access the value stored at the address. Clearly the instruction only makes sense in the long version, and the form LEA is equivalent to LEA.L. It is good practice to always specify the length of each instruction explicitly because different instructions default to different lengths.

The LEA instruction is important, because the reference to the label LAB above can be made using program counter relative addressing, which ensures that the instruction is position independent. LEA should always be used to load the address of a location in your program, while the immediate form of MOVE should be used to load immediate data items.

LEA can also be used to perform simple sums which are done as part of address evaluation. For example,

```
LEA      20(A3),A3
```

will evaluate the effective address specified by 20(A3). This is the contents of A3 plus the constant 20, which is then placed into A3. The effect is to add 20 to A3. Any control addressing mode is allowed, so that another example would be

```
LEA      20(A2,D1.L),A3
```

which will load A3 with the sum of the constant 20, the contents of A2 and the contents of D1. Although addresses are normally only 24 bits long the entire 32 bits of an address register are altered in this way.

A cousin of LEA is called PEA, for Push Effective Address. This instruction evaluates the address given as the source in the same way as LEA, but instead of placing the resulting effective address into an address register, it stores it on the stack. In fact this action is performed as part of BSR and JSR, where the effective address of the next instruction is stored on the stack. We could even simulate the effect of BSR as follows.

```
        PEA.L   NEXT        Save return address on stack
        BRA     SUBR        Branch to subroutine
NEXT    ....    Return to here
```

Here we push a return address onto the stack, and then use BRA rather than BSR to enter a subroutine. When the subroutine returns using RTS it will pick up the saved address on the stack, and return to the instruction labelled NEXT, which in this case happens the be next instruction after the subroutine call. Here we simulated the action of BSR, but of course the address specified to PEA does not have to refer to the instruction after BRA, and could refer to anywhere.

PEA can also be used in elementary sums, so that

```
        PEA.L   20(A3)      Save A3 + 20 on stack
        MOVE.L  (SP)+,D0    Load D0 with saved value
```

will save the contents of A3 plus 20 on the stack, and then read this value off the stack and into D0. This is one possible way of obtaining the effect of an LEA instruction using a data register as the destination.

Allocating stack space

In previous examples we have seen how the stack may be used to hold return addresses, saved copies of registers and temporary results. However in all of these cases we have to remove items from the stack in the opposite order to that in which they were placed there. It is often useful to be able to allocate an area of memory where results are saved, and to be able to read or write to these locations whenever we wish.

One way of doing this is to use absolute memory locations, but again we come up against the problems of position independence; we would have to reserve a particular memory area for our program to use. Although we might go to some lengths to ensure that the program can be placed anywhere in memory, this is no use if the data areas are tied to a specific location. We could reserve areas of memory within the program space, and refer to these using program counter relative addressing. However we can only read memory locations specified in this way, as the architecture of the 68000, quite rightly, discourages the writing of programs which overwrite themselves.

Another solution is to use an address register, and to ensure that it points to an area of memory which can be used to hold results. We reserve offsets from this address register and use them to store our data. So if A1 points to our data space, we could refer to locations as follows.

```
DATA1   EQU    0            Data area offsets
DATA2   EQU    4
        ...    Set up A1
        MOVE.L #20,D1        Get value
        MOVE.L D1,DATA1(A1) Save in data area
        ...
```

This works reasonably well, but we have two problems. The first is concerned with allocating the data space. We will have to use an operating system call to obtain some free space and initialise A1 to point to it. Such operating system calls can be rather expensive, but an example of a suitable free space allocation package is given in chapter 6. The second problem is that we will have to allocate this space every time we enter a subroutine which needs a data area, so that any subroutine can call any other. To avoid eating up all the space, we will also have to ensure that we give the space back whenever we exit from a subroutine.

The solution is to take the space we need for permanent data from the stack. Up to now we have only considered allowing the stack to grow when we actually place a data item onto it. Thus a subroutine might be called which saves one register, and then calls another subroutine. The stack will contain the return address for the second subroutine, then the saved register and return address from the first subroutine.

Now consider allocating part of the stack as a data area. When we enter the first subroutine we immediately save our register, so that the stack contains the saved register value and the return address. We now set up our data area pointer A1 so that it is the same as the stack pointer A7, and alter A7 so that sufficient space is allocated beyond A1 for our needs. When we call the second subroutine the return address will be stored at the stack position indicated by A7, out of the way of our data area.

The second subroutine is now free to save registers and to allocate its own data area on the stack if required. It will have to save the old contents of register A1 before it can allocate a new work area, and restore the stack and all the registers when it has finished.

This may sound rather complicated, but in fact it is very easy and the. 68000 provides special instructions to help us. Before we learn about these, let us review what a subroutine should have to do when it is entered and when it is left. These two sections of code are called the entry and exit sequences.

Entry sequence

1) On entry, A7 points to return address and A1 points to previous data area.

2) Save any work registers used. A7 points to to saved registers and return address, A1 points to previous data area.

3) Save old value of A1 on stack and load A1 with A7, so that it points to a new work area. Decrement A7 by size of required work area, remembering that the stack runs from high memory to low memory.

The resulting stack frame will be as follows.

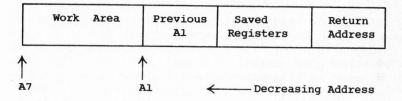

Work Area	Previous A1	Saved Registers	Return Address

↑ A7   ↑ A1   ←——— Decreasing Address

Exit sequence

1) Load A7 with value of A1, thus deallocating work area. A7 now points to the saved values of A1, any work registers and the return address. Reload previous value of A1 from stack.

2) Restore saved values of work registers from stack. A7 now points to the return address and all other registers have their original value restored.

3) Load return address from the stack and jump to it.

We can now try to turn this into 68000 assembly code. Stage 1 of the entry sequence is performed by the calling subroutine using BSR or JSR. Stage 2 is performed by a MOVE or, more usually, MOVEM onto the stack using predecrement address mode. Stage 3 is peformed all in one operation by the LINK instruction. This saves the address register specified as the source on the stack, then loads it with the (updated) value of A7. Finally it adds the immediate value given as the destination to the stack pointer A7. Because the stack runs down memory we must use a negative value as the displacement.

Once in the subroutine proper we can use negative offsets from A1 as our data locations, so long as we do not use any offsets which are beyond the current value of A7. It is important that sufficient work space is reserved by specifying a large enough displacement to the LINK instruction. If offsets are used which extend below the top of the stack they will be corrupted by any further subroutine calls.

The exit sequence is just as simple. Stage 1 is performed by UNLK, which is the opposite of LINK. The stack pointer A7 is loaded from the register specified as argument, and then this register is loaded from the top of the stack. Stage 2 is another MOVE or MOVEM using postincrement addressing mode from the stack pointer. Finally stage 3 is simply RTS.

```
* Standard entry sequence
        MOVEM.L D0-D7/A0,-(SP) Save work registers
        LINK    A1,#-32         Allocate 8 long words
        ...
* Perform work, using -4(A1) to -32(A1) for data
* Possibly call other subroutines
        ...
* Standard exit sequence
        UNLK    A1              Deallocate workspace
        MOVEM.L (SP)+,D0-D7/A0 Restore registers
        RTS     Return to caller
```

This arrangement is often used by implementors of high level languages, especially those which work with a stack such as Pascal or Ada. If you want to write a subroutine which is callable from a high level language you must ensure that it conforms to the standard used by subroutines in that particular language. Inevitably there will be some variations in the actual scheme used in different implementations.

A memory check example

We have now learnt enough about the 68000 to be able to write a complete program. It will not be terribly exciting, but will contain examples of some of the instructions met so far.

The program will check that the memory locations in a certain range do in fact work as expected – in other words that the memory really does remember. Because of the way in which hardware is organised memory faults often appear as certain store locations always returning a 0 or 1 in a particular bit position. Just writing a zero into memory and checking that this remains the same is not good enough, as such a check will not trap a bit always returning zero. In fact some faults are only evident when a particular pattern is written into the offending location, so an exhaustive check should be done on memory using all possible bit combinations.

The first part of the program will handle the output of information to the terminal. The subroutine WRCH will write out the character stored in register D0.

```
A_CTRL   EQU      $840021        ACIA control port
A_DATA   EQU      $840023        ACIA data port

WRCH     BTST     #1,A_CTRL      Test for port ready
         BEQ.S    WRCH           Loop until it is
         MOVE.B   D0,A_DATA      Transmit character
         RTS
```

We can now define the subroutine WRITES which will write out a string. The string is pointed at by register A1 and is terminated by a byte containing zero.

```
WRITES   MOVEM.L  D0/A1,-(SP)    Save registers
WRS1     MOVE.B   (A1)+,D0       Extract character
         BEQ.S    WRS2           Zero byte - exit
         BSR.S    WRCH           Write character
         BRA.S    WRS1           Get next character
WRS2     MOVEM.L  (SP)+,D0/A1    Restore registers
         RTS                     And return
```

For each possible . bit pattern we want to write the value into all memory locations within the specified range. Once this has been done we must then run through memory again checking the value has not changed. It is not sufficient to check immediately after writing as the action of writing to one address may alter another location unexpectedly. However the . loop is identical in each case – it is only the action to be performed which changes.

A rather neat way to accomplish this is to have a subroutine which runs through memory. For each address it calls another subroutine to perform the required action. The first subroutine will be called SCAN, and register A2 will contain the address of another subroutine to do the required action. The register D0 will contain the current test bit pattern and A0 will point to the location under test. Both of these registers will be used by the two possible subroutines addressed by A2, and A0 will be incremented by one each time these subroutines are called.

```
SCAN     MOVE.L   A0,-(SP)       Save A0
         MOVEA.L  #MEMLO,A0      Start of test area
SCN1     JSR      (A2)           Call routine to do work
* A0 is incremented by subroutine called
         CMPA.L   #MEMHI,A0      Check if loop finished
         BNE.S    SCN1           No .. carry on
         MOVE.L   (SP)+,A0       Restore A0
         RTS                     And return
```

The two subroutines called by SCAN are simple. The first simply places the value held in D0 into the location addressed by A0 and increments A0.

```
WRITE    MOVE.B  D0,(A0)+      Store value
         RTS
```

The second checks that the value held in D0 is the same as that held in the memory location addressed by A0. It increments A0 and writes a message if the memory is not as expected.

```
READ     CMP.B   (A0)+,D0      Check memory
         BEQ.S   RD1           Same, return
* Memory not the same, so we must write error message
         MOVE.L  A1,-(SP)      Save previous A1
         LEA.L   MESS3,A1      Point to error message
         BSR.S   WRITES        And write it out
         MOVE.L  (SP)+,A1      Restore old A1
RD1      RTS
```

The final stage is to write the main part of the program. We will assume that the ACIA has already been initialised for us by the monitor or operating system. During the execution of the program we will keep the current test value in register D0. This will be initialised to $FF. and we will use DBcc to control the loop for all possible bit patterns. We use a word length instruction to perform this initialisation because DBcc decrements the entire bottom 16 bits of a register. We will also keep A1 pointing to a message which we will print out once round the loop as a reminder that the program is indeed working.

```
MEMLO    EQU     $4000         Start memory address
MEMHI    EQU     $8000         End memory address
CR       EQU     $0D           ASCII return
LF       EQU     $0A           ASCII line feed

MCHECK   LEA.L   MESS1,A1      Get initial message
         BSR.S   WRITES        Write message
         LEA.L   MESS2,A1      Get progress message
         MOVE.W  #$FF,D0       Set up initial value for test
* Start of loop changing test pattern
LOOP     BSR.S   WRITES        Write progress message
         LEA.L   WRITE,A2      Point to WRITE subroutine
         BSR.S   SCAN          Scan memory performing WRITE
         LEA.L   READ,A2       Point to READ subroutine
         BSR.S   SCAN          Scan memory performing READ
         DBRA    D0,LOOP       Decrement test pattern
* Test complete. Write another message
         LEA.L   MESS4,A1      Point to message
         BSR.S   WRITES        Write it
         RTS                   Return to main program
* Messages
MESS1    DC.B    'Memory check starting',CR,LF,0
MESS2    DC.B    'Pass completed',CR,LF,0
MESS3    DC.B    'ERROR detected',CR,LF,0
MESS4    DC.B    'Memory check complete',CR,LF,0
         END
```

Chapter 5

Arithmetic

We have so far managed to discuss a large number of the instructions of the 68000, and have not yet mentioned any way of performing arithmetic. This is not accidental – most computers spend much more time moving and comparing data than they ever do performing sums. The idea of a computer simply being a complicated calculating machine is extremely old-fashioned.

Addition

We have, in fact, already learnt how to perform simple addition, as the 68000 will add while it is evaluating addresses. We have already learnt how the LEA and PEA instructions can be used to add values, so long as at least one of the values is in an address register. While this is a useful trick, the most common arithmetic operations take place on the data registers.

The name of the addition instruction is, not surprisingly, ADD. Like so many of the 68000 instruction set, there is a whole family of ADD instructions.

The basic ADD instruction must be used with a data register as either the source or the destination. If the data register is the destination, then any addressing mode may be used. If the data register is the source, then the destination must be specified using a memory alterable address mode. The operation can take any of the sizes byte, word or long unless the source is an address register, in which case only word and long sizes are allowed.

The operation affects the condition codes according to the result. The N and Z bits are set if the result is negative or zero respectively, and cleared otherwise. The V bit is set if an overflow is generated, and cleared otherwise. The C and X bits are both set or cleared depending on whether a carry is generated.

The ADD instruction can be used to alter just the low order 16 or 8 bits of the destination data register. Its cousin, ADDA, is used to add values in address registers. Like MOVEA, ADDA does not affect any of the condition codes and can only be used as length word or long. If the word version is used this only affects the size of the source value, which is sign extended to 32 bits and added to the entire 32 bits held in the destination address register. Again this is a trap for the unwary, as adding a word value with the most significant bit set will cause a negative value to be added to the destination.

The source for ADDA can also be specified using any address mode, but again there is a special version of the instruction for adding immediate data. The ADDI instruction takes an immediate value as source, and any data alterable addressing mode as the destination. This means that ADDI cannot be used to add immediate data to an address register, but could be used if the destination was a data register, although the ADD instruction could also be used in this case.

ADDI is used to add constant values to memory locations. It can take any of the three sizes, and sets the condition codes in the same way as ADD. However, one of the most popular values to add is one, so that some location or register is incremented each time round a loop, for instance. Some instruction sets provide a special 'increment' operation, but the 68000 goes further. The ADDQ (for ADD Quick) instruction can be used to add a number between 1 and 8 to any alterable address. This is very useful – for example it is common to add four to a register which is acting as a pointer.

The ADDQ instruction behaves just like ADDI, except for two points. Firstly, it is shorter, and so should be used in preference to the ADDI form, particularly when the long size is used. The condition codes are set in exactly the same way as ADDI in this case. The second difference is that ADDQ can be used with an address register as the destination, in which case it acts just like ADDA with immediate data. In this case the only sizes allowed are word or long, (although whichever is used is irrelevent as the entire address register is altered), and the condition codes are not affected.

The final member of the ADD family is ADDX (ADD eXtended). This comes in two distinct flavours, depending on whether the operands are a pair of data registers or a pair of memory locations specified by address registers in predecrement mode. In either case the instruction can be of length byte, word or long.

The ADDX instruction is used to add two values together just like ADD, but it also adds in the X bit. This will normally be set or unset by some other arithmetic operation immediately before the ADDX is used, and allows multiple precision arithmetic to be performed. Notice that the X bit is set to the same value as the C bit in arithmetic operations, but is not affected by other instructions such as MOVE which may alter the C bit.

The condition codes are set in the same way as in the ADD instruction with one exception. This is the Z bit, which is cleared if the result is non-zero in the normal way. However it is unchanged, as opposed to set, if the result is zero. This is normally used in multiple precision operations. The Z bit is set before a number of ADDX instructions which make up a multiple precision operation. If any of the intermediate results are non-zero then the bit will be cleared, and will be clear at the end of the complete operation. If however the Z bit is still set at the end, then all the intermediate results were zero, and so the entire multiple precision result is zero.

Subtraction

The SUB family has exactly the same members as those described above for ADD. The basic SUB operation has a data register as source or destination, and sets the condition codes. This time, of course, the C and X bits are set if a borrow is generated.

SUBA is used if the destination is an address register, and the condition codes are not affected. SUBI is used if the source is immediate data, and SUBQ can be used if the immediate data is in the range 1 to 8. Again it should be remembered that if word sized values are used with SUBQ and the destination is an address register, then the word value is sign extended before it is used.

SUBX is also available, which takes the contents of the destination, subtracts the source, then subtracts the X bit and places the result in the destination. Again the operands can only be a pair of data registers or a pair of address registers in predecrement mode, and the Z condition code is cleared if the result is non-zero and unchanged otherwise.

Although the full range of instructions are described here, many assemblers will automatically make the choice between the correct form of the instruction where possible. It is important to make the distinction if code is being generated without an assembler, such as in a compiler.

Negating values

Any value can be negated by the NEG instruction. This simply subtracts the destination from zero. The operation can be of size byte, word or long and the destination can be specified using any data alterable addressing mode.

If the result is zero then the Z condition code will be set and the C and X bits will be cleared. If the result is non-zero then Z will be unset and C and X will be set. N and V will be set or cleared depending on whether the result is negative or an overflow occurs respectively.

There is only one variant of the NEG instruction and that is NEGX. This negates the value specified and then subtracts the X bit from it. The condition codes N and V are set in a similar way to NEG. Z is cleared if the result is zero but unchanged otherwise, in a similar fashion to ADDX and SUBX. C and X are set or cleared depending on whether a borrow is generated. This instruction is normally used when negating multiple precision values held in more than a single long word.

Multiplication

The addition and subtraction instructions of the 68000 are complete, in the sense that they can operate on all three possible sizes of operand. Unfortunately this is not true of multiplication or division. The only size of instruction allowed for these two arithmetic operations is word. Preliminary information from Motorola indicates that long versions of these instructions will be available in the 68020.

There are two multiplication operations available, called MULS and MULU. The only difference is that the first performs signed arithmetic and produces a signed result, while the second performs unsigned arithmetic and produces an unsigned result.

Both instructions take any data addressing mode as the source operand, and a data register as the destination. The content of the low order 16 bits of the destination register is multiplied with the word value indicated by the source address. If this is a memory location then the value is 16 bits starting at that memory location. If the source is a data register then the value is the low order 16 bits of the register.

The result is placed as a 32 bit number in the destination register. The N and and Z bits are set if the result is zero or negative as usual; for the unsigned case 'negative' means if the top bit is set. V and C are always cleared, and X is unaffected.

Swapping register values

A useful instruction to introduce here is SWAP. This simply takes a data register and exchanges the top 16 bits with the bottom 16. It is very useful when providing long multiplication and division routines and fighting with the 16 bit operations provided.

The condition codes are set by this instruction. The N bit is set if the most significant bit in the resulting 32 bit data register is set, and cleared otherwise. Notice that the bit which is tested is the one which was the most significant bit in the low order word before the operation. The Z bit is set or cleared depending on whether the entire register is zero or not. V and C are always cleared, while X is not affected.

There are two other instructions which can be usefully introduced here. The first is EXG, which simply exchanges the values stored in two registers. The two registers may be both address or data registers, or they may be one of each type. The entire register contents is exchanged, so the operation is only of type long. The condition codes are not affected.

The other instruction is EXT, which is used to sign extend the value of a data register. The instruction is only available as size word or long. If size word is used, the high order bit of the low order byte is transferred to bits 15 to 8 in the register. If size long is specified then the high order bit of the low order word is copied into the high order word.

For example, EXT is required if a byte value representing a signed number is loaded into a register prior to addition to a word or long sized operand. If the addition was to be done using size word, then an EXT.W would be required to set the word value in the register as a signed number. If an addition of size long was to be performed an EXT.L operation would be required as well. The first EXT would set the word representation correct, while the second would correct the long representation. In many cases sign extension from word to long is performed automatically in the course of other instructions, particularly where address registers are concerned.

The X condition code is not affected by the EXT operation. V and C are always cleared while N and Z are set or cleared depending on the whether the result is negative or zero.

Long multiplication

Because of the lack of a long multiplication operation, we need to provide a subroutine to do the job. This will take two 32 bit quantities and produce a 32 bit answer. Obviously if we attempt to multiply two large 32 bit numbers the result will overflow; in this first example we will ignore any possible overflow.

In order to perform the multiplication we must first remember how we do long multiplication by hand. Those of you who do not always use a calculator will remember the algorithm used to multiply two decimal numbers together when each number contains two digits. Most of us can multiply any two single digit numbers together in our heads, but may have to resort to pencil and paper for anything more complicated. Consider multiplying two numbers AB and CD, where each letter represents a single decimal digit. We might proceed as follows:

```
            A        B
            C        D
         -----------
         D*A      D*B
   C*A   C*B
         -----------------
   C*A  D*A+C*B  D*B
         -----------------
```

Because we can always multiply any single digit number with any other, we split the multiplication into simpler multiplies and additions. The highest digit is the result of multiplying the highest order digits together, while the lowest digit is the result of multiplying the lowest order digits. The remaining digit in the answer is the sum of the cross terms. Obviously we must remember to handle overflow when the result of a simple multiply is a two digit number – this is done by carrying over the extra digit into the next column.

This algorithm is exactly what is required for our long multiplication routine. The 68000 can always execute multiplies on any two 16-bit numbers, so we split the long multiplication into multiplies which we can perform, along with some additions. We consider each 32-bit number as consisting of two 16-bit digits, represented as RH and RL if the number is held in the 32-bit register R. We can then use the method described above, ignoring for the time being the overflow third digit represented by C*A above. Thus if the two numbers are initially held in registers D1 and D2, the result will be given as

```
RL  =  D1L * D2L
RH  =  (D2H * D1L) + (D1H * D2L) + carry from RL
```

Let us now try to turn this into 68000 code. We will write a routine which multiplies the two numbers held in registers D1 and D2, placing the result in D1.

```
MUL      MOVEM.L D2-D4,-(SP)  Save registers
         MOVE.W  D1,D3        D1L into D3
         MOVE.W  D2,D4        D2L into D4
         SWAP    D1           D1H into D1
         SWAP    D2           D2H into D2
* Create the products
         MULU    D3,D2        D2 = D1L*D2H
         MULU    D4,D1        D1 = D2L*D1H
         MULU    D4,D3        D3 = D2L*D1L
* Add cross terms ignoring overflow
         ADD.W   D2,D1        D1 = D2L*D1H+D1L*D2H
* Place cross term into high digit of .result
         SWAP    D1           D1H = cross term
         CLR.W   D1           Clear D1L
* Insert bottom digit
         ADD.L   D3,D1        D1L and D1H now correct
         MOVEM.L (SP)+,D2-D4  Restore registers used
         RTS
```

Here we must remember that the MULU instruction takes two 16-bit values and produces a 32-bit result. The first line saves registers used, while the next four break up the input numbers into four 16-bit units. The high order word of the registers will be ignored by MULU, so it does not matter what they contain. The MOVE.W instructions only affect the low order word, and we use the SWAP instruction to place the high order word into the low order part of a register.

The next three lines produce three 32-bit results as products from the 16-bit input values. We then· use an ADD.W instruction to add the cross products together. This may well cause an overflow, which we ignore. This 16-bit sum is moved into the high order word of the result register D1, and the low order word is cleared.

The final action required is to insert the low order word of the result into the correct place in the result register. However this cannot be done by a MOVE.W from D3 into D1, as we must allow for a carry from the low order digit to the high order one. The product of D1L and D2L is held in the high order word of D3. A simple ADD.L of D3 and D1 ensures that the low order word is correctly inserted into the answer. Again any overflow generated by this instruction is ignored.

The next routine will take two 32-bit numbers in registers D1 and D2 and will produce a 64-bit result in the register pair D6,D7. In other words, D6 will hold the most significant part of the answer and D7 will hold the least significant part. We must extend the algorithm used to obtain the result as follows:

```
D7L = D1L * D2L
D7H = (D2H * D1L) + (D1H * D2L) + carry from D7L
D6L = D1H * D2H + carry from D7H
D6H = carry from D6L
```

We shall have to make use of the X bit which indicates whether a carry has been generated during an arithmetic instruction.

```
LMUL    MOVEM.L D3/D4,-(SP)  Save registers
        MOVE.L  D1,D3
        MOVE.L  D2,D4
        SWAP    D3           D3 = D1H
        SWAP    D4           D4 = D2H
* Create products
        MOVE.W  D1,D7        D7 = D1L
        MULU    D2,D7        D7 = D2L*D1L
        MOVE.W  D3,D6        D6 = D1H
        MULU    D4,D6        D6 = D2H*D1H
        MULU    D1,D4        D4 = D1L*D2H
        MULU    D2,D3        D3 = D2L*D1H
* Add cross products together
        ADD.L   D3,D4        X bit relevant now
* Handle low order part of cross product
        MOVE.W  D4,D3        D3L = D4L
        SWAP    D3           D3H = D4L
        CLR.W   D3           Clear D3L
* Handle high order part of cross product
        CLR.W   D4           Clear D4L
        ADDX.W  D3,D4        Set D4L to state of X bit
        SWAP    D4           D4 = high 17 bits of cross product
* Add low order cross terms in D3H to D7
        ADD.L   D3,D7        X bit relevant
* Add high order of cross terms in D4
        ADDX.L  D4,D6        Include carry from previous ADD
* D6,D7 now holds unsigned 64-bit product
        TST.L   D1           Check D1 negative
        BPL.S   LMUL1        Branch if not
        SUB.L   D2,D6        Subtract D2 from answer
LMUL1   TST.L   D2           Check D2 negative
        BPL.S   LMUL2        Branch if not
        SUB.L   D1,D6        Subtract D1 from answer
LMUL2   MOVEM.L -(SP),D3/D4  Restore registers
        RTS
```

The first few lines of this routine save the work registers D3 and D4, and then place the high order words of the operands into the low order words of the work registers.

The next lines create the product terms. The lowest order digit of the answer is going to be placed in D7, so it is computed immediately. Similarly the highest order digit is placed in D6. We use the work registers D3 and D4 to hold the two cross products. These are then added together to give a 32-bit result in D4, with the X bit indicating whether a carry has been generated. We must take care to add the X bit to D6 later on.

The next lines handle the cross product. The low order word of the cross product must be placed in the second digit position of the result, which is D7H. We must also include the carry digit from the low order product which is held in D7H. We therefore move D4L into D3L, swap register halves and clear the low order word to give us the low order word of the cross product in D3H. In a moment this will be added to D7, but we cannot do this yet because that will affect the X bit which still indicates whether a carry was generated when the cross product terms were added.

The high order part of the cross product is to be placed in the bottom half of a work register prior to being added to D6. We must also take care of the X bit now. The bottom half of D4 is cleared with a CLR.W, and the X bit is placed into D4L. This might possibly be done by an ADDX with an immediate argument of zero, but ADDX can only be used with two data registers or two address registers in predecrement mode. We therefore use ADDX.W on D3 and D4, noticing that D3L just happens to have been cleared to zero two instructions previously. Once this has been done D4H contains the high order digit of the cross product, and D4L contains 0 or 1 depending on the state of the X bit. A simple SWAP now ensures that D4 contains the high order 17 bits of the cross product.

We are now nearly home and dry. Adding D3 to D7 ensures that the two low order digits of the answer are correct, with the X bit set if there is a carry pending from D7 into D6. An ADDX.L of D4 to D6 adds this carry bit and the high order part of the cross product into the high order product generated earlier, leaving us with the 64-bit result in D6 and D7.

This works fine for positive numbers, but we have in fact performed an unsigned multiplication on the input values. This means that if we intended to multiply −1 by 2, for example, we have in fact multiplied $FFFFFFFF by $2 using unsigned arithmetic. This will give us D6 containing $1 and D7 containing $FFFFFFFE; this is not the value −2 which we would expect if performing signed arithmetic.

The correction for this is simple, and is based on the fact that we are using two's complement arithmetic. Thus −A is represented by the value M−A, where M is 2 raised to the power 32. Hence

$$(-A) * B = (M-A) * B = (M*B) - (A*B)$$

Therefore the unsigned product of a negative number A and a positive number B will be the same as the signed product plus M*B. However it is very simple to perform the multiplication M*B, as it simply entails shifting the 64-bit representation of B 32 places to the left. As B is held in a single 32-bit register, and the answer is held in the register pair D6,D7 we simply subtract the value of B from the high order register of the answer, which is D6. The original operands are still held in registers D1 and D2, so if D1 was originally negative then we must subtract D2 from D6. If D2 was negative we must subtract D1 from D6. This correction then completes our signed arithmetic routine.

Division

We stated earlier that the 68000 did not have long forms of multiplication or division. There are two division instructions provided which handle signed and unsigned division. They both take a word sized value as the source, which can be specified using any data addressing mode. The destination must be a data register of size long. The entire 32-bit value held in this data register is divided by the word value specified as source. The DIVU instruction performs this divison using unsigned arithmetic, while the DIVS instruction uses signed arithmetic.

In both cases two results are produced. The low order word of the destination is set to the quotient, assuming that it will fit into a word. The high order half is set to the integer remainder. In the case of DIVS this remainder will have the same sign as the numerator.

The N and Z status bits are set or cleared as usual depending on whether the quotient is negative or zero. The C bit is always cleared and the X bit is unaffected. If the resulting quotient is larger than a 16-bit value then overflow will be detected and the V bit will be set. However the detection of overflow may occur while the 68000 is in the middle of processing the instruction. In this case the result and hence the state of the N and Z bits will be undefined. The TRAPV instruction, described in chapter 7, can be used to cause a trap if overflow has in fact occurred. If the source is zero then a 'division by zero' trap will occur.

Long division

Because DIVS and DIVU will only work if the result is less than 16 bits, we are also going to need a long division routine. This is a little more difficult than the long multiplication routine described earlier. The following routine is due to Dr. Arthur Norman, and divides a 32-bit numerator held in D1 by a 32-bit denominator in D2. The 32-bit quotient is returned in D1 with D2 holding the integer remainder.

The first section handles the sign, so that the main work can be done using unsigned arithmetic. First we check to see if the denominator is negative. If it is then we make it positive, perform the division and then reverse the sign of the answer.

```
DIV     TST.L   D2          Check denominator < 0
        BPL.S   DIV00       No
        NEG.L   D2          Make denominator positive
        BSR.S   DIV00       Do division as if positive
        NEG.L   D1          Now negate the answer
        RTS                 And return
```

This next case deals with a negative numerator but a positive denominator. Here we must convert the numerator to positive, perform the division and then reverse the sign of both the quotient and the remainder.

```
DIVOO    TST.L    D1           Check numerator < 0
         BPL.S    DIVU         Both operands positive
         NEG.L    D1           Make numerator positive
         BSR.S    DIVU         Perform division
         NEG.L    D1           Correct sign of quotient
         NEG.L    D2           Correct sign of remainder
         RTS                   Complete
```

The next section deals with division of unsigned numbers where D1 and D2 are greater than or equal to zero and less than or equal to $80000000. If D2 is actually equal to zero then a 'divide by zero' trap will occur. In order to avoid performing too much work we check for a number of easy cases. The first of these is the situation where the denominator is less than 16 bits, and hence we can use the standard DIVU instruction. If this is the case then we jump to a standard subroutine DIVX which does the division and sets the remainder correctly.

```
DIVU     CMPI.L   #$FFFF,D2    Test if D2H is zero
         BLS.S    DIVX         D2 < 16 bits, use subroutine
```

At this stage we check for two other special cases. If the numerator is less than the denominator then the answer is zero, and if they are equal the quotient is 1.

```
         CMP.L    D1,D2        Check if D2 <= D1
         BEQ.S    DIVO1        D1 = D2, simple case
         BLS.S    DIVO2        Difficult case
* Here D1 < D2, so the result is zero
         MOVE.L   D1,D2        Get remainder correct
         MOVEQ    #0,D1        Zero result
         RTS
* Here D1 = D2, so the result is 1
DIVO1    MOVEQ    #0,D2        Zero remainder
         MOVEQ    #1,D1        Result is 1
         RTS
```

The more general case is where the denominator is larger than 16 bits. As the numerator fits into 32 bits the resulting quotient will be a 16-bit object. We produce an approximation to the required quotient by dividing both the numerator and the denominator by a scale factor which is chosen so that the scaled denominator will fit into 16 bits. We can then perform a standard division on the new scaled operands. We must choose a scale factor which will itself fit into 16 bits, and which will produce a suitably accurate approximation. We actually use 1+(D2/$10000) as the scale factor, which we note will always fit into 16 bits because the largest value we allow D2 is $80000000, thus ensuring that the largest possible scale factor is $8001.

```
DIVO2    MOVEM.L D3-D5,-(SP)    Save work registers
         MOVE.L  D2,D3          Save denominator
         CLR.W   D3             Clear D3L
         SWAP    D3             D3 = D2 / $10000
         ADDQ.L  #1,D3          D3 = 1 + (D2/$10000)
* Scale factor in D7. Scale numerator and denominator
         MOVE.L  D1,D4          D4 = numerator
         MOVE.L  D2,D5          D5 = denominator
         MOVE.L  D3,D2          Scalefactor into D2 for DIVX
         BSR.S   DIVX           D1 = D1 / Scalefactor
         MOVE.L  D5,D2          Replace denominator
         DIVU    D3,D2          D2L = D2 / Scalefactor
* D2 should now fit into 16 bits
         DIVU    D2,D1          Divide scaled terms
```

At this point D1L contains an estimate for the quotient we are looking for. We check the result by multiplying the approximation to the quotient by the original denominator and comparing this with the original numerator. We can also produce the remainder at the same time. If the quotient is not correct we either add or subtract one and try again until the result is correct.

```
         ANDI.L  #$FFFF,D1      D1H = 0
DIVO3    MOVE.L  D5,D2          Restore original denominator
         MOVE.L  D5,D3          Into D3 as well
         SWAP    D3             D3L = D2H
         MULU    D1,D2          D2 = D1*D2L
         MULU    D1,D3          D3 = D1*D2H, D3H is zero
         SWAP    D3             Move into high digit
         ADD.L   D3,D2          Get product, no carry possible
         SUB.L   D4,D2          Subtract original numerator
         BHI.S   DIVO4          Overshot, remainder negative
         NEG.L   D2             Change sign
         CMP.L   D2,D5          Compare with original denominator
         BHI.S   DIVO5          OK, remainder is in range
         ADDQ.L  #1,D1          Increment quotient
         BRA.S   DIVO3          Try again
DIVO4    SUBQ.L  #1,D1          Decrement quotient
         BRA.S   DIVO3          Try again
* Got it!
DIVO5    MOVEM.L (SP)+,D3-D5    Restore registers
         RTS
```

The only operation left now is the specification of the subroutine DIVX. This is used if the original quotient fits into 16 bits, and is also called to scale the numerator in the more difficult case. It sets D1 to the original value of D1 divided by D2, and sets D2 to the integer remainder. Note the use of MOVEM.W to save the low order words of D1 and D3. We do not use MOVEM.W to restore the registers partly because it is convenient to pick them off one by one, but mainly because MOVEM.W will alter the entire contents of registers if used to restore them.

```
DIVX      MOVEM.W D1/D3,-(SP)    Save D1L and D3L
          CLR.W   D1            Clear D1L
          SWAP    D1            D1 = D1H
          DIVU    D2,D1         D1L = D1H/D2
          MOVE.W  D1,D3         Save partial result
          MOVE.W  (SP)+,D1      Retrieve D1L
* D1H holds D1H rem D2, D1L as on entry
          DIVU    D2,D1         D1L = (D1L+(D1H rem D2))/D2
          SWAP    D1            D1L now holds remainder
          MOVEQ   #0,D2         Clear D2
          MOVE.W  D1,D2         Remainder into D2
          MOVE.W  D3,D1         D1L = high order quotient
          SWAP    D1            Swap to get 32bit quotient
          MOVE.W  (SP)+,D3      Restore D3L
          RTS                   All done
```

Decimal arithmetic

The preceding discussion has been about performing arithmetic on binary values – that is numbers held in two's complement binary form. Arithmetic on such quantities is fast, but it is rather awkward to convert between decimal values as read by humans and binary values as read by computers.

Some high level languages such as COBOL provide the programmer with the ability to choose whether operations are to be performed in decimal arithmetic or binary arithmetic. The advantage of using binary is that sums are quick, but the conversion process from decimal to binary is slow. The advantage of using decimal arithmetic is that it is very quick and easy to read values into the machine in decimal form from decimal input; conversly the disadvantage is that the sums are slow.

The 68000 provides three instructions which can be used to perform decimal arithmetic. They are ABCD (Add Binary Coded Decimal), NBCD (Negate Binary Coded Decimal) and SBCD (Subtract Binary Coded Decimal). They all work on a byte value which represents two decimal digits stored in Binary Coded Decimal or BCD. Each 'nibble', or 4 bits, is used to hold a decimal value between 0 and 9. Thus the decimal number 16 will be stored as $10 in binary form, and will be stored as $16 in BCD.

Normally a number will be read in from some external medium in decimal form a character at a time. In order to convert the entire decimal number to binary we must use a routine such as the following.

```
RDN     MOVEQ   #0,D1           Clear total
        MOVE    D1,D0           Clear all of D0
RDN1    BSR     RDCH            Get character in D0
        SUB.B   #'0',D0         Subtract character 0
        BMI.S   RDN2            Negative - no more digits
        CMP.B   #9,D0           Check valid digit
        BGT.S   RDN2            No more digits
        MULS    #10,D1          Multiply old total by 10
        ADD.L   D0,D1           Add this digit to total
        BRA.S   RDN1            Get next digit
RDN2    RTS                     Return with total in D1
```

This routine assembles the binary version of a decimal number read from some external source — the subroutine RDCH is used to obtain information a character at a time. The character is checked to be a valid digit and converted to the binary equivalent. The previous value of the total is multiplied by 10, and the new digit added to the total. This routine will only read a number which fits into a word, and would have to be adapted to call the long multiplication subroutine if larger numbers were required. A process just as complex must be followed in order to convert a number into decimal again so that it may be written out.

This all takes time, and it may be the case that the only action to be done to the numbers obtained in this way is to add them to some other value. An example might be reading through a long list of figures adding them all together. We could write a routine to do this, using our subroutine to read the decimal number and convert it to binary.

```
COUNT   MOVEQ   #0,D4           Grand total in D4
        MOVE.W  #4,D5           5 numbers to read
CNT1    BSR.S   RDN             Get number in D1
        ADD.L   D1,D4           Add to total
        DBRA    D5,CNT1         Get next number
```

In this case using decimal arithmetic might be better. We will have to use memory locations to hold the two numbers involved. The following routine reads a number and places the result in BCD form in an eight byte area addressed by A1. We shall assume that we are reading the numbers from a right justified field of sixteen characters, so that the number read exactly fills the BCD area. If this was not the case we would have to clear the area before we read the number. Leading blanks will be treated as zero, and we shall not check that the field only contains digits and spaces. The routine will return with A1 pointing to just beyond the BCD area.

```
DRDN    MOVEM.L D0/D1,-(SP)  Save registers
        MOVEQ   #7,D1        Initialise counter
DRDN1   BSR     RDCH         Get character
        ASL.B   #4,D0        Move up to high nibble
        MOVE.B  D0,(A1)      Place in memory
        BSR     RDCH         Get next character
        AND.B   #$F,D0       Mask to low nibble
        OR.B    D0,(A1)+     Install in memory
        DBRA    D0,DRDN1     Loop until all done
        MOVEM.L (SP)+,D0/D1  Restore registers
        RTS     Return
```

The first few lines save registers and initialise a counter. A call to RDCH then returns with the character representation of a decimal digit or a space held in D0. In ASCII the digits are hexadecimal $30 to $39, and space is $20. If we only look at the bottom four bits we will get the correct value for the number so long as the field only contains spaces or numbers. We assume this is the case and shift the character representation left by four bits, clearing the bottom nibble and setting the top nibble to the value of the decimal digit. This is then stored at the current value of A1.

A further call to RDCH returns the next digit or space. This time we AND the value with $F to clear the top nibble, and then OR the result into memory to fill the bottom nibble in the stored version. We use postincrement addressing so that A1 now points to the next byte. When we have finished A1 will end up pointing to eight bytes higher in memory, and the storage area will contain the BCD representation of the number. Note that this number can be larger than that which can normally be stored in 32-bit binary form.

The next routine uses ABCD to add decimal numbers together, in the same way that we used ADD in the earlier example to add binary numbers.

```
SIZE    EQU     8            Number of bytes to hold each number
COUNT   LINK    A0,#-SIZE*2  Allocate room for two numbers
        LEA.L   -SIZE(A0),A1 Set A1 to top of second area
* Set first area to BCD zero
CNT1    CLR.B   -(A1)        Decrement A1 and zero byte
        CMPA.L  A7,A1        Check if end of first area reached
        BNE.S   CNT1         Continue until all cleared
        MOVE.W  #4,D5        Set up counter
* This loop perfoms the totalling
CNT2    LEA.L   -SIZE(A0),A1 Set A1 to base of second area
        MOVEA.L A1,A2        Set A2 to top of first area
        BSR.S   DRDN         Read number
* A1 and A2 now point to the end of decimal values
        SUB.B   D0,D0        Clear X bit
CNT3    ABCD    -(A1),-(A2)  Add two bytes
        CMPA.L  A7,A2        Finished yet?
        BNE.S   CNT3         Continue
        DBRA    D5,CNT2      Loop until all done
```

The first part of this program allocates some workspace from the stack. This is going to be sufficient for two numbers, and for the purpose of this example we will assume that the total will fit into eight bytes. We use the first area for the total and the second area for the current number.

The first small loop sets all the bytes in the total to zero, noting that A7 marks the limit of available memory. The first two instructions in the main loop which does the totalling simply reset A1 to the start of the input value area and A2 to just after the result area. Once the number has been read by DRDN A1 will point to just after the number in the input area.

The next loop will add the input number to the result using decimal arithmetic. The state of the X status bit is very important here, as ABCD adds the source and destination together and also includes the X bit. The X bit is set if a decimal carry is generated, so the repeated additions will work correctly. Before the loop is started we must clear the X bit, and so we subtract the byte contents of D0 from itself to ensure that this is clear. We will see later how the X bit can be cleared more elegantly.

Each time round the loop one byte each from the two decimal values are added together along with the X bit. If a decimal carry is generated then the C and X bits will reflect this the next time round. The Z bit will be cleared if any of the bytes are non-zero, but will not be affected if the result is zero. We have set the Z bit by means of the SUB instruction so that once the entire addition loop is complete the Z bit will be set only if all the bytes were zero. In this case we could, if we wished, test the Z bit to perform some action only if the result was zero. The other two condition codes (N and V) are undefined after an ABCD instruction. The X bit is unaffected by the CMPA instruction which sees if we have completed the loop yet.

You will notice that we have used address register predecrement mode for both of the operands to ABCD. This is one of only two allowed address modes, the other being both data registers. The memory version is normally the most useful, and it must take predecrement mode as that is the order in which the bytes must be added. The data register case simply allows the individual bytes to be placed in the two registers; in either case the instruction is of size byte.

The SBCD instruction is very similar. Again it can only take the same two address modes, and the destination byte will contain the original decimal value of the destination less the decimal value of the source and the X bit. The condition codes are altered in the same way except that C and X are set if a decimal borrow is generated.

The final decimal instruction is NBCD, which may be used to negate decimal values. In fact the NBCD instruction is similar to NEGX, as the destination byte is negated · and the X bit then subtracted from it. The condition codes are set in the same way as in SBCD. Unlike the previous two instructions, any data alterable address mode may be used as the operand to NBCD.

Although not a decimal operation, the CMPM instruction which we met earlier is often useful when handling decimal arithmetic. It can only be used with the postincrement addressing mode, but is useful to compare two decimal numbers held in memory to see if they are equal.

Our final requirement when handling decimal arithmetic is to write out a number stored in BCD. Such a routine would be the opposite of the DRDN subroutine described earlier. It is passed a pointer to the start of a BCD storage area in A1 and prints the number out using WRCH. A1 is left pointing to just past the end of the area. This simple example prints out all leading zeros; a more sophisticated version would convert leading zeros to spaces.

```
DWRN    MOVEM.L DO-D2,-(SP)    Save registers
        MOVEQ   #7,D1          Initialise counter
        MOVEQ   #12,D2         Set up shift value
DWRN1   MOVE.L  #$30300,DO     Set up DO
        MOVE.B  (A1)+,DO       Extract two decimal characters
        ROR.W   #4,DO          Move nibbles around
        BSR     WRCH           Print first digit
        LSR.L   D2,DO          Shift down other character
        BSR     WRCH           Print second digit
        DBRA    D1,DWRN1       Loop
        MOVEM.L (SP)+,DO-D2    Restore registers
        RTS                    And return
```

The main loop of this routine firstly sets DO to the value $30300, for reasons which will become apparent. We then extract a byte from the BCD area which contains two decimal digits to be printed, and place this in the low order byte of DO. Thus if the byte contained $56, DO will now contain $30356.

The ROR.W instruction rotates the low order word by four bits, thus placing the lowest nibble in the top half of the bottom word and shifting the rest of this word right by four. In our example DO will now contain $36035. The low order byte now contains $35, which is the ASCII representation of the number '5', and which is written out by a call to WRCH.

The LSR.L instruction wishes to shift the entire contents of DO right by twelve places. The amount to shift can only be expressed as an immediate value if it is less than eight places, so we have to use D2 which we have previously initialised to 12. This will move the value $36 into the low order byte in our example, which is the ASCII value of '6'. This is then written out and we loop back if required to print all the digits.

The contortions which we have to go through to convert to and from character form and BCD are indeed faster than the equivalent conversions to and from binary, but in many machines instructions called something like 'pack' and 'unpack' are provided. These convert from one form to the other in one simple instruction. In fact early documentation on the 68000 mentioned just these instructions. We are now promised PACK and UNPK in the 68020.

Chapter 6

Logical operations

In the previous chapters we have seen how the patterns of bits in registers and memory locations can be regarded as representing numbers or characters, and manipulated appropriately. Binary representation is used in computers because it is much easier to make reliable electronic devices which have just two states (e.g. 'on' and 'off') than ones which have more. Although the precise way in which numbers and characters are stored is usually unimportant, it is nevertheless sometimes useful to take advantage of binary representation, and to manipulate values regarding them just as collections of bits. Such manipulations are called **logical** operations to distinguish them from arithmetic operations. A single bit can be thought of as having the logical value **true** or **false** rather than 1 or 0.

Perhaps the simplest logical operation is that of inverting every bit of the operand.

```
NOT.L    D3
```

will convert every 1 bit in D3 to a 0, and vice versa. In common with the other logical instructions, NOT is allowed only on data alterable operands; this reinforces the convention that address registers are intended only for holding addresses, and that logical operations on addresses are likely to be symptomatic of an incorrect or deviously-written program. However, it is sometimes useful to be able to perform bit manipulation on addresses, as we shall see in the store allocation routines later in this chapter.

There are several logical operations which take two operands. They differ from arithmetic operations in that the corresponding bits of each operand are combined separately, rather than treating the whole byte or word as a single value. It is like performing a set of 8, 16 or 32 one-bit calculations in parallel.

The **OR** operation produces a result with a bit set in every position where either the source **or** the destination has one set. If the low byte of D1 is 11001100 in binary, and that of D2 is 11100001, then

        OR.B   D1,D2

will leave D2 containing 11101101 in its low byte. Another way of thinking about OR is to say that ORing with 0 leaves a bit unchanged, while ORing with 1 always sets it. Thus we can set the more significant half of a register to 1s without disturbing the rest by using

        OR.L   #$FFFF0000,D3

A complementary way of combining bits is by ANDing them. The result of an AND operation has 1-bits only in the positions where both the first **and** the second operand had 1s. Using the same values in D1 and D2 as above

        AND.B   D1,D2

will leave D2 with 11000000 in its least significant byte. AND is the inverse of OR in the sense that ANDing with 0 gives 0, while ANDing with 1 leaves the bit unaltered. The AND instruction is useful for **masking** part of a value: that is, setting the unwanted bits to zero without affecting the rest. Suppose we have just done some calculation which leaves an 8-bit result in the low byte of D4, but makes no guarantee about the state of the other bits. We can clear these bits so that the value of the whole of D4 is just the wanted result by writing

        AND.L   #$000000FF,D4

The third instruction provided for combining two sets of bits is the **exclusive-or** (EOR) instruction. This gives a 1 in the result where the two operand bits are different; where they are both 0 or both 1, the result is 0. If, once again, D1 contains 11001100 and D2 holds 1110001, then

        EOR.B   D1,D2

will put 00101101 in D2.

Another view of this operation is that EOR with 0 leaves a bit unchanged, while EOR with 1 inverts the bit. Thus EOR with all 1s is equivalent to NOT.

The form of operands allowed for EOR is slightly different from those of AND and OR, as the source must be a data register. The other two must have a data register as at least one of the operands, but it can be source or destination. All three instructions have an immediate form (ANDI, ORI, and EORI) for use when the source is a constant bit pattern (though an immediate source operand can be used with the ordinary AND and OR forms as well). A peculiarity of these instructions is that the destination may be the status register (SR). If the operation size is byte, then only the low order byte of the status register is affected: this is the condition code register (CCR). If the size is word, then the whole status register is used, and the operation is privileged. These forms of the three instructions enable particular status and condition code flags to be set (ORI), cleared (ANDI), or inverted (EORI), without affecting other bits. For instance, to clear the carry flag we would write

```
ANDI.B  #$FE,CCR
```

and to set trace mode we could say

```
ORI.W   #$8000,SR
```

Shifting and rotating

We have seen how individual bits may be manipulated in place, and will now see how to move bit patterns about within a register or store location. There are four types of instruction for doing this, and each has a version for moving left and one for moving right. All of the shift instructions take three forms of operands. The operand can be in memory, in which case the operation size is always word, and the shift is by one bit. If the operand is in a data register then all three operation sizes are allowed, and the shift may be either by a fixed amount (1 to 8 bits), or by a number given in another data register.

The **logical shift** instruction LSL moves to the left all the bits in its operand, and introduces 0s on the right. Suppose that the word of memory addressed by A1 contains 1011111111111111. The effect of

```
LSL.W   (A1)
```

is to set this word to 0111111111111110. The carry (C) and extend (X) condition codes are set from the lost bit, and the N and Z flags are set in the normal way from the result value.

As mentioned above, a value in a data register may be shifted by more than one bit at once, and the number of places may be specified in two ways. A constant shift of 1 to 8 bits is expressed as immediate data, as in

```
LSL.L   #4,D2
```

Alternatively, the shift count can be given in another data register:

```
LSL.L   D1,D2
```

The count used is the value in the register modulo 64.

The LSR instruction performs rightwards logical shifts, bringing in zeros from the left, and setting the C and X flags from the last bit shifted off the right hand end.

When we shift a binary number one bit to the left, the effect is to multiply its value by two. Shifting one place to the right is like dividing by two and throwing away the remainder. Thus we can use shifting as a way of multiplying and dividing by powers of 2 (2, 4, 8, 16, etc.). We could use the LSL instruction for multiplying in this way, but using LSR for division would not give the correct answers with negative numbers. Zeros would be shifted in on the left, unsetting the sign bit.

To get round this problem, two more shift instructions are provided. These are the arithmetic shifts ASL and ASR, which assume that their operand is a number in twos-complement form. They take exactly the same operand formats as LSL and LSR, but differ from those instructions in the treatment of the sign bit and condition codes. For left shifts, the difference is subtle: LSL always clears the V (overflow) condition code flag, while ASL sets it if arithmetic overflow has occurred, and clears it otherwise. The final bit pattern in the operand location or register is the same for both instructions.

The different handling of the sign bit affects right shifts only. The bits shifted in from the left are copies of the original sign bit, ensuring that ASR will have the effect of division for both positive and negative numbers. For positive numbers, LSR and ASR have identical effects, but for negative numbers, ASR will shift in 1s rather than 0s from the left. For example, if the least significant byte of D1 is 11101100 (= −20 in decimal), then the effect of

```
ASR.B    #2,D1
```

is to set this byte to 11111011 (= −5 in decimal). Any fractional part of the result is of course lost, meaning that the result of division will be truncated towards minus infinity. Thus

```
 5 shifted right by 1  =    5/2  =  2
-5 shifted right by 1  = (-5)/2  = -3
```

Both arithmetic and logical shifts lose bits which fall off the end of the operand. An alternative is to use the **rotate** operations (sometimes called **circular shifts**), in which bits moved out of one end of the operand are reintroduced at the other end. Thus no information is lost, and shifting sufficient times (e.g. 8 for a byte) will restore the operand to its original state.

There are two kinds of rotate instruction. Both take the same forms of operands as the other shift instructions, and have left and right variants. ROL and ROR rotate the operand value by the specified amount, and leave in the C flag a copy of the last bit which was taken round from one end to the other. The N and Z flags are set from the result value, V is always cleared, and X is unaffected. ROXL and ROXR are very similar, except that each bit shifted out goes into the X flag, and the bit introduced at the other end is the old value of X. These instructions will take one more step to restore an operand than the simple rotates (e.g. 9 steps for a byte). Their importance lies in the fact that they are the only shift operations which allow the value of the bit which is brought into the operand to be determined by a previous instruction. Thus, they can be used for shifting objects larger than 32 bits. For example, if we had a 64-bit quantity in D1 and D2, we could do a logical left shift of the whole thing by writing

```
LSL.L    #1,D2        LS half: lost bit goes into X
ROXL.L   #1,D1        MS half: get bit from LS half from X
```

Converting a hexadecimal number to characters

We can use the logical operations that we have seen so far to write a piece of code which will convert a number held in a register into the characters of its hexadecimal representation. Each hexadecimal digit corresponds to four bits of the number, sometimes called a nibble (half a byte!). We can use a rotation to bring each nibble in turn to the least significant end of a register, and then mask with an AND operation. This gives us a number from 0 to 15 which can be used to select the appropriate character from a table of sixteen.

```
* The number to be converted to characters is in D1
* A0 points to an eight-byte buffer for the character form

        MOVEQ    #7,D0        Use D0 as loop count

LOOP    ROL.L    #4,D1        Get next nibble to bottom of D1
        MOVE.B   D1,D2        Copy two lowest nibbles
        ANDI.L   #$F,D2       Mask low nibble
        MOVEA.L  D2,A1        Need it in address register
        MOVE.B   CHARTAB(A1),(A0)+ Put corresponding character in
*                             next buffer position and step
        DBRA     D0,LOOP      On to next nibble

* Exit here: conversion complete

        : :
        : :

CHARTAB DC.B     '0123456789ABCDEF' Conversion table
```

Operations on single bits

Five instructions are available for operating on single bits in a data register or byte of memory. One of them, TAS, is rather special, and will be dealt with later. The other four, BTST, BCLR, BSET, and BCHG, form a family which all take the same operand formats. Each of these four operates on a single bit, and the position of that bit is specified by its number in the memory byte or register operand. Bits are numbered from zero upwards, starting from the least significant (or right hand) end of the operand. Thus a register has bits numbered 31 to 0, and a byte has bits from 7 to 0.

The BTST instruction simply tests the specified bit, and sets the Z flag to its value; no other condition code flag is affected. The bit number can be given either as an immediate value, or in a data register. The destination operand may be of any data addressing mode, except the immediate addressing mode. If the operand is a data register, then the bit numbering is taken to be modulo 32. This means that the number used is the remainder when the specified number is divided by 32, so the two instructions

```
BTST    #3,D7          and
BTST    #35,D7
```

would both test bit number 3 of D7. When the operand is a byte of memory, the bit number is taken modulo 8.

The other three instructions in this family also test the specified bit, but they may also alter it, and so must have a destination operand of a data alterable addressing mode. BCLR clears the bit to 0, BSET sets it to 1, and BCHG gives it the opposite value from the one it had before.

Since memory is organised in bytes, a bit operation must read a whole byte, alter one bit within it, and then write it all back. This means that using BCLR, BCHG, or BSET to alter bits in memory-mapped peripheral control registers may have unexpected effects, as the action of reading the location may itself cause some action in the peripheral device. It is safer to construct the required bit pattern and then use MOVE to set such control registers.

The 'test and set' (TAS) instruction also affects just one bit in its operand. It is less flexible than the other bit instructions, as its length attribute is always 'byte', and it is always bit 7 of the byte which is tested and then set. Both the N and Z flags are set from the original value of the operand byte. TAS can be used with any data alterable operand, but its importance lies in the way it accesses a byte in memory. It uses what is called a 'read-modify-write' memory cycle. This means that TAS retains control of the memory for the whole time it is executing, so that nothing else can look at or alter the operand byte while TAS is inspecting and setting it. As mentioned in chapter 1, this is a vital operation in a system where several computers share the same memory, as it enables them to use flag bytes in memory to indicate whether or not resources that they all share are currently in use. Such flags are called **semaphores**. It is necessary that each computer should be able to set a semaphore and find out whether it was set before, in a way that prevents the other computers from altering the flag during this operation.

Semaphores can also be needed within a single computer, if that computer contains several programs running more or less independently. Many operating systems allow several programs to be active at once, and arrange to share out the processor's time between them. Even in a simpler system, the code of interrupt routines (see chapter 7) can run at random times during the execution of the main program. In a single computer, BCLR, BCHG, and BSET (as well as TAS) can be used for handling semaphores, as they all do a 'test and set' type of operation in a single instruction. This means that no program can alter a semaphore while another is in the process of looking at it and setting it.

A free store allocation package

In simple programs, it is usually possible to predict in advance how much data storage will be required for the various data structures, buffers, and so on, and to divide up the available memory accordingly. However, many programs need to be able to split the total store between different uses, and the amounts needed for some structures may not be known until the program is actually run. In these cases it is useful to have some mechanism for reserving areas of store, and for releasing them again when they are no longer needed. Such a mechanism can be provided as a collection of routines forming a **store allocation package**.

A simple package contains just two routines: one for allocating memory, and another for releasing it. One way to organise the store is as follows. Assuming that all the available store is in one contiguous region, it is possible to divide it up into blocks, placed end to end. Each block has a header word which indicates firstly the length of the block, and secondly, whether it is free or in use. The very last block consists of just a header word containing zero.

We will make a rule that all blocks are a multiple of 4 bytes in length, and have headers which are long words. This allows the size of a block to be as large as the memory on any 68000 system, and also ensures that we will never get left with any gaps between blocks into which we cannot fit a header. We will also insist that all blocks start at even addresses, so that the headers can be manipulated with instructions of size long. Since all lengths are multiples of 4, the least significant two bits of a length will always be zero. We can therefore use the least significant bit as a flag to say whether or not the block is free.

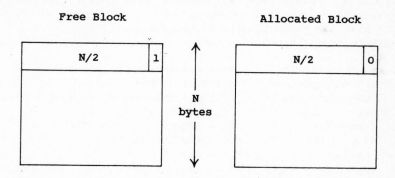

Free Block   Allocated Block

The total size of each kind (including its header) is N bytes.

The routine which allocates store is called GETBLK. It uses a 'first fit' algorithm for allocating memory: i.e. it works its way through the blocks and allocates from the first free one which is large enough. It joins together any adjacent free blocks that it passes on the way. After a while, when many blocks have been obtained and then freed again, it is quite likely that some free blocks will be next to each other. It would be silly to reject a later GETBLK request simply because no single free block was big enough, but there is no need to do the work of combining adjacent ones until such a request is made.

```
*               GETBLK
*
*   Routine to allocate an area of store
*
*   Entry:  D1 = number of bytes required
*
*   Exit:   A0 = address of first byte of allocated block,
*                or zero if allocation failed·
*           D0 = error code: 0 = block allocated
*                            1 = insufficient free store
*                            2 = block list found to be corrupt


GETBLK  MOVEM.L  A1/D1-D3,-(SP) Save work registers
        ADDQ.L   #3,D1          Add 3 to number of bytes wanted
        ANDI.B   #$FC,D1        Round to multiple of 4
        ADDQ.L   #4,D1          Block size = (rounded) size + 4
        BLE      GBC7           Error if negative

GBCRTY  LEA.L    BLKLIST,A0     Get start of store chain

* Search down the chain for a free block and
* amalgamate any adjacent free areas.

GBC1    MOVE.L   (A0),D2        D2 = size+marker of block
        BLE.S    GBC6           End of list (or error)
        BCLR.L   #0,D2          Test the marker and clear it
        BNE.S    GBC2           Jump if the block is free
        ADDA.L   D2,A0          A0 = address of next block
        BRA.S    GBC1           Continue down list

* Have found a free block

GBC2    MOVE.L   A0,D3          D3 = address of free block
*
GBC3    ADDA.L   D2,A0          A0 = address of next block
        MOVE.L   (A0),D2        Get size and marker of next block
        BMI.S    ERRSTORE       Jump if loop in free store
        BCLR.L   #0,D2          Test the marker and clear it
        BNE.S    GBC3           Jump if block free - carry on if
*                               allocated (or end of chain reached)
```

```
* Now D1 = size required in bytes
*      D3 = address of start of free area
*      A0 = address of end of area
* Amalgamate the group of free blocks

GBC4      MOVE.L   A0,D2         Copy end address
          SUB.L    D3,D2         D2 = amalgamated size in bytes
          BSET     #0,D2         Set free marker
          MOVEA.L  D3,A1         Get start in address register
          MOVE.L   D2,(A1)       Amalgamate free blocks
          BCLR     #0,D2         Unset free marker for arithmetic
*
          SUB.L    D1,D2         Split block (D2 = size of excess)
          BLT.S    GBC1          Can't be done
          BEQ.S    GBC5          Exact fit

* Must make new block for upper part

          SUBA.L   D2,A0         A0 = address of upper part
          BSET     #0,D2         D2 = size of upper part + marker
          MOVE.L   D2,(A0)       Plant in upper block
*
GBC5      MOVE.L   D1,(A1)       Plant the size (marker bit zero)
          ADDQ.L   #4,D3         D3 = address of allocated space
          MOVEA.L  D3,A0         Put in result register
          CLR.L    D0            No errors
          BRA.S    GBEXIT        Return

* Error or end of store chain reached

GBC6      BMI.S    ERRSTORE      Loop in store chain

* Not enough free store for request

GBC7      MOVEQ    #1,D0         Insufficient store code
GBERREX   SUBA.L   A0,A0         Clear result register
GBEXIT    MOVEM.L  (SP)+,A1/D1-D3 Restore work registers
          RTS      Return

* Error exit

ERRSTORE  MOVEQ #2,D0 Corrupt store chain code
          BRA.S    GBERREX       Take error exit
```

The routine for giving back a block of allocated store is called FREEBLK. Its job is very simple, as all it has to do is to set the least significant bit of the header word, in order to mark the block as being free. However, it can do some simple checks in order to be reasonably sure that the address it has been given is indeed that of a block previously allocated by GETBLK. The supplied address is checked for being even (as we made the rule that all blocks start at even addresses), and the flag bit in the header word is inspected to make sure the block was allocated. The most common programming error is freeing a block twice, and this simple test will detect that.

FREEBLK also checks that neither address nor header has any bits set in the most significant byte. We have not gone in for more elaborate (and time consuming) checks such as scanning down the whole list of blocks to make sure that the address really does refer to an allocated block.

FREEBLK returns immediately if it is given zero as its argument. This ensures that the result of GETBLK is always a valid argument to FREEBLK, even if the former fails to allocate any store.

```
*         FREEBLK
*
* Free store allocated by GETBLK
*
* Entry: D1 = block address
*
* Exit:  D0 = 0  Block freed
*            = 1  Does not appear to be an allocated block

FREEBLK MOVEM.L D1/D2/A0,-(SP) Save work registers
        CLR.L   D0              Set 'ok' result
        TST.L   D1              Look at block address
        BEQ.S   FBEXIT          Return if zero

        SUBQ.L  #4,D1           Point at block header word
        MOVE.L  D1,D2           Copy the header address

* Inspect address given: it should be even, and should
* have no bits set in the top byte.

        ANDI.L  #$FF000001,D2 Check address is of form
*                             0000 0000 dddd ... ddd0
        BNE.S   FBERR           It isn't

        MOVEA.L D1,A0           Get into address register
        MOVE.L  (A0),D2         Look at first word of block
        ANDI.L  #$FF000001,D1 Check header is of form
*                             0000 0000 dddd ... ddd0
        BNE.S   FBERR           It isn't

        BSET    #0,3(A0)     Set 'free' marker bit
FBEXIT  MOVEM.L (SP)+,D1/D2/A0 Restore work registers
        RTS

FBERR   MOVEQ   #1,D0           Error result
        BRA.S   FBEXIT          Return
```

The initial free store chain, consisting of one (large) free block, followed by a zero word, could be set up as follows:

```
BLKLIST DC.L    BLKEND-BLKLIST+1 Size + 'free' marker
        DS.L    1000            Some free store
BLKEND  DC.L    0               End marker
```

Chapter 7

Exception handling

In all the program examples we have seen so far, the address of the next instruction to be executed is determined (implicitly or explicitly) by the instruction currently executing. Usually it is just the next instruction in sequence, but a branch, jump, or return instruction can force execution to continue elsewhere.

This chapter is about the situations when control is diverted in other ways: these situations are called **exceptions**. There are two purposes for which exceptions are used. One is to enable action to be taken rapidly when some event occurs, such as a user pressing a key on his terminal keyboard. The other purpose is to provide the computer with a means of reporting that some error has been detected, and calling a routine to take appropriate action. An example is when an illegal instruction is encountered.

When an exception is processed, the 68000 saves the current values of the program counter and status register, and then continues execution at an address given in an **exception vector** at a low memory address. The saved information enables execution to be resumed later at the point where it was interrupted; the effect is like calling a subroutine between two instructions.

Exceptions can be generated in two ways: either **internally** when the processor itself detects some anomalous situation, or **externally**, when some other hardware needs to gain the processor's attention. External exceptions are usually called **interrupts**, while internal ones are often called **traps**.

The external exceptions are

    Interrupts
    Bus error
    External reset

The internal exceptions are caused by

Illegal instructions
Unimplemented instructions
Address error
Privileged instructions in user state
Tracing
Divide by zero
TRAP, TRAPV, CHK

Exception Vectors

When an exception occurs, the processor calls a routine provided by the user to handle that exception. We have to give it a way of finding the address of that routine. On some computers, the same routine is called for any exception, and its address is held in some fixed store location. This routine must start by inspecting some system registers to find out what actually happened.

The 68000 has a more general scheme which allows a separate routine to be provided for each **type** of exception, and for each external device. The lowest 1024 bytes of memory are reserved for holding the addresses of all these routines. Each address is held in a 4-byte slot known as an **exception vector**. Each vector has a number, which is just its byte address divided by four. The position and number of the vectors is given in the following table.

The exception vector number is implicit for all internal traps and for external interrupts which use the auto-vector mechanism. Circuitry which causes other interrupts must present a vector number to the 68000; the choice of vector number is up to the designer.

If the three function code output lines from the 68000 are being used to separate the memory into distinct address spaces, then all but the reset vector will be taken from the supervisor data space. The reset vector will be taken from the supervisor program address space.

Vector Number	Address (Hex)	Type of Exception or Interrupt
0	0	Reset: Initial SSP
1	4	Reset: Initial PC
2	8	Bus Error
3	C	Address Error
4	10	Illegal Instruction
5	14	Division by zero
6	18	CHK instruction
7	1C	TRAPV instruction
8	20	Privilege violation
9	24	Trace Exception
10	28	Unimplemented instruction (1010)
11	2C	Unimplemented instruction (1111)
12 : to 23	30 : 5C	(Unassigned, but reserved by Motorola for future expansion)
24	60	Spurious Interrupt
25	64	Level 1 Interrupt Auto-vector
26	68	Level 2 Interrupt Auto-vector
27	6C	Level 3 Interrupt Auto-vector
28	70	Level 4 Interrupt Auto-vector
29	74	Level 5 Interrupt Auto-vector
30	78	Level 6 Interrupt Auto-vector
31	7C	Level 7 Interrupt Auto-vector
32 : to 47	80 : BC	TRAP #0 instruction TRAP #15 instruction
48 : to 63	C0 : FC	(Unassigned, but reserved by Motorola for future expansion)
64 : to 255	100 : 3FF	User interrupt vectors

User and supervisor states

As mentioned in chapter one, the 68000 can execute instructions in either user state or supervisor state. The two states correspond to different levels of privilege. Supervisor state is the more privileged, and programs forming part of an operating system should normally run in this state. Any instruction may be executed while in this state. User state is used for running all other programs. Several key instructions are forbidden in this state, and any attempt to execute them will cause a trap which will pass control back to the operating system. The instructions which are disallowed fall into two categories: those which could interfere with the operation of the computer, such as STOP and RESET, and those which would allow the program to enter supervisor state but continue executing its own instructions.

The processor chip has an output line which signals the current state. This can be used in two ways to protect memory belonging to the supervisor. It could be checked on each memory access in the hardware in order to forbid access to certain regions while in user state. The other way it could be used would be to completely separate the memory available to the supervisor from that available in user programs. Thus address 1000 when in user state would access a different memory location to address 1000 in supervisor state. In this way, the private supervisor memory would be invisible to user programs.

Address register 7 is special, as it is used implicitly as a stack pointer by some instructions and during exceptions and interrupts. It is also peculiar in that the name corresponds to two physical registers, the user stack pointer (USP) and the supervisor stack pointer (SSP). The one accessed by a reference to A7 depends on the processor state. The name SP is sometimes used for the current stack pointer. Thus SSP is not accessible in user state. However, there is a special instruction which gives access to USP in supervisor state, as an operating system will need to be able to read and set this register. This instruction is a special case of the MOVE instruction, with USP as either source or destination. It is privileged, not for reasons of protection, but because any program which does use it in user state is doing something silly.

The only way that the state can change from user to supervisor is when a trap or interrupt occurs. This means that the change is always associated with a jump to a address determined by the **trap vectors** in low store. By protecting this store from access in user state, it is possible to ensure that it is impossible to enter supervisor state without also jumping to a system program, and thus restrict what user programs are able to do.

There are several ways of returning from supervisor to user state. The supervisor is allowed to execute those instructions which directly update the processor status register (SR), so can simply negate the bit which controls the state. It can also set user state as part of returning from an exception via the RTE instruction (see below).

How exceptions are processed

The action taken by the processor is similar for all the different kinds of exception. In all cases, the current values of the program counter and status register are saved, so that the interrupted program can eventually be resumed as if nothing had happened. They are saved in three words of the system stack, as shown

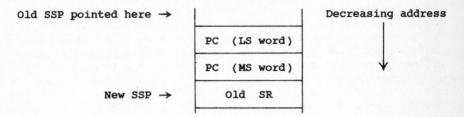

Old SSP pointed here → 　　　　　　　　　Decreasing address

PC (LS word)

PC (MS word)

New SSP → 　Old SR

Note that it is always the **supervisor** stack which is used (i.e. that pointed to by SSP rather than USP), regardless of which state the processor was in when the exception occurred. The address error and bus error exceptions save more information than this (see below). In most cases, the saved program counter points at the instruction which would have been executed next if the exception had not happened. Note that the 68010 and 68020 processors save one more word on the stack which contains the exception vector number. This makes it easier to share the same code to handle different exceptions.

The status register is set to a standard state after the old version has been saved. The supervisor state bit is set on so that the exception handling routine will always start in supervisor state. The Trace bit is turned off, so that exceptions can be taken normally even when the main program is being traced (see below). The 3-bit interrupt mask is affected only by the reset exception, and by interrupts. Reset sets this mask to 7, while an interrupt sets it to the priority level of that interrupt (see below).

Routines to handle exceptions

A program which is going to handle exceptions will start by inserting in the exception vectors the addresses of the routines which are to be called when each exception occurs. The skeleton layout of an exception routine is as follows

```
ENTRYPT MOVEM.L Dp-Dq/Ar-As,-(SP) Save any regs used below
        :
        :                       Take action necessary to
        :                       handle exception
        :
        MOVEM.L (SP)+,Dp-Dq/Ar-As Restore all saved regs
        RTE                     Return to interrupted program
```

An exception can occur at an arbitrary time, between any pair of instructions. In order to be able to resume properly, it is essential to preserve the original status register, and the contents of all the address and data registers. The status register is saved automatically, but it is the job of the handler routine to make sure it does not corrupt any other registers. The easiest way to do this is to use MOVEM to save on the stack any registers which are used in the routine, and to use it again at the end to get them all back.

The RTE instruction does the rest of the work of returning from an exception handler. It expects the old program counter and status register to be on the stack in the order shown above, and restores both of them, thus resuming the program that was interrupted. The action of RTE is similar to

```
MOVE.W   (SP)+,SR
RTS
```

However, it cannot be replaced by these two instructions, as RTE always pops the program counter from the **supervisor stack**, whereas RTS takes it from the user or supervisor stack, according to the current processor mode. If the MOVE.W to SR instruction changed the mode from supervisor to user, then RTS would operate on the wrong stack.

Note that use of RTE is forbidden in user state, as it allows the status register to be set directly, and so would provide an uncontrolled means of getting into supervisor state.

An unprivileged instruction very similar to RTE is RTR. It too sets the program counter and status register from values on the stack, the only difference being that it sets only the **user** byte of the status register (the half containing the condition codes). It takes a whole word of stack for the status register, but only the low byte is actually used. Thus RTR is like the sequence

```
MOVE.W   (SP)+,CCR
RTS
```

One use of RTR is as an alternative to RTS in a subroutine which preserves the condition codes present when it was called. Such a subroutine would have the form

```
SUBNAME MOVE.W  CCR,-(SP)      Save cond codes
        :
        :
        :
        RTR                    Restore cond codes and return
```

Another use for RTE, RTR, and RTS is as jump instructions. To use JMP to go to an address that was not known at the time the program was written, we must hold that address in an address register. If we want to jump somewhere, having set **all** the registers to particular values, we can do so by putting the destination address on the stack and using RTS.

```
MOVE.L   destaddr,-(SP) Store destination address
  :
  :                      Set all registers
  :
RTS                      Jump
```

RTR or RTE can be used like this to set up the condition codes, or (in supervisor state) the whole status register, before jumping.

Interrupts

Interrupts are the means by which external devices request action from the processor. A device requests an interrupt by presenting a priority level between 1 and 7 to the processor. The interrupt will be accepted only if the current processor priority level (held in the status register) is less than the interrupt level, or if the requested level is 7. Level 7 thus acts like a **non-maskable interrupt** (NMI) on other computers. The logic which requests the interrupt must also indicate whether it will supply a vector number, or whether **auto-vectoring** should be used. This means that the processor uses a vector from the range 25 to 31, according to the requested priority level. A vector number is normally supplied when many devices interrupt at the same priority level.

The processing of an interrupt follows the normal sequence for an exception, with the program counter and status register being saved on the stack, and the status register being set to a standard state. The saved program counter points to the instruction which would have been executed next if the interrupt had not occurred. The priority level in the status register is set to the level of the interrupt. The purpose of this is to prevent further interrupts of the same or lower levels, but to allow ones of higher priority. Some computer peripherals need fast response to an interrupt request, otherwise data may be lost, whereas for others there is less, or no, urgency. The designer of a computer system can choose the interrupt priorities in such a way as to guarantee to give rapid servicing to the interrupts for which it matters. Interrupts of the same or lower levels than the current one are inhibited in order to simplify the programming of the interrupt routines. If the inhibition were not there, then an interrupt service routine could be interrupted and the same routine called again. This would cause chaos if the routine thought it had exclusive use of any memory locations or ports.

External reset

A reset exception can be caused by circuitry outside the processor. This is used to start the processor initially, or to restart it after some crash which cannot be recovered from in any other way. All record of what was going on at the time of the reset is lost.

Reset differs from all other exceptions in two ways. Firstly, nothing is saved on the stack, as the stack pointer may not refer to a valid address. Secondly, the exception vector is eight bytes long (rather than four), and contains the initial value of the system stack pointer as well as the new program counter.

Illegal and unimplemented Instructions

If the 68000 attempts to execute a word which does not contain a valid instruction, then it will cause a trap to occur, saving a program counter value which points to the offending word. One of three exception vectors is used.

If the most significant four bits of the word are 1010 or 1111, then the instruction is considered to be **unimplemented** rather than illegal. These groups of instructions are ones which may be assigned meanings in future models of the 68000, or for which separate **co-processor** chips may be provided. Unimplemented instructions provoke traps to one of two vectors, according to these four bits. This is to allow emulation of unimplemented instructions in software. Given the specification of an instruction, an exception handling routine can be written to have precisely the same effect as that instruction, albeit rather more slowly. This means that is is possible to provide software so that programs containing unimplemented instructions (perhaps written for a later version of the 68000) can be run unchanged.

Illegal instructions which fall into neither of these groups cause a trap through the 'illegal instruction' vector. Encountering this trap is a symptom of either a wild jump (e.g. indirecting through an address register that had not been initialised), or of running off the end of a program into data or unused memory.

Instructions which can cause traps

Some instructions can cause traps as part of their normal execution, either because that is their main job, or because some abnormal condition can arise during their execution.

The TRAP instruction always causes an exception. Its operand is a number from 0 to 15, and one of sixteen exception vectors is used accordingly, so there is, in effect, a family of sixteen TRAP instructions. It has a variety of uses. The major use is as a call to an operating system or monitor. As has been explained earlier, in a protected system it is necessary to run the operating system code in supervisor state so that it can restrict the actions of user programs (which run in user state). The TRAP instruction allows programs to call subroutines in the operating system, and to put the processor into supervisor state as part of the call. The reason for the call can be conveyed either by the operand of the TRAP, or by an argument in a register.

Another use for TRAP is for setting breakpoints in a debugging program. As it is only two bytes long, it can be substituted for the first word of any instruction. When the program gets to that point, an exception will be taken, diverting control back to the debugger, which will then print a message to its user. The monitor in the next chapter provides a breakpoint facility in just this way.

Two other instructions cause a trap if a particular condition is true. They are both intended as cheap tests for errors which may occur when a program is running, and could be inserted automatically at all appropriate points by a compiler for a high level language. TRAPV forces an exception if the V condition code is set. If a TRAPV is inserted after every arithmetic operation in a program, then an exception will occur whenever there is overflow. For example, we might have a sequence of code like

```
ADD.L    (A1),D4
TRAPV
ASL.L    #2,D4
TRAPV
```

The other of these instructions is CHK, which is designed for checking that access to an array of store is within the range of that array. CHK compares the value referenced by its first operand to the low 16 bits of the data register which is its second operand. If the value in the data register is less than zero or greater than the first operand, a trap occurs. Suppose A1 contains the address of an array of bytes, D1 contains the offset of the one we want to update, and the word addressed by A2 holds the upper bound of the array. CHK could be used as follows

```
CHK      (A2),D1        Check that offset is in range
MOVE.B   VALUE,0(A1,D1.W) Update array byte
```

Two more instructions which can force exceptions are those for division, DIVU and DIVS. Both of these will trap if they are asked to divide by zero.

When any of the above instructions provokes an exception, the saved program counter points to the next instruction in sequence.

Privilege violations

We mentioned earlier that some instructions may be executed only when the processor is in supervisor state. These instructions are all the ones which would enable a program to steal control of the computer from the operating system, by updating the status register, or resetting the peripherals. The following instructions are privileged

```
RESET
STOP     #xxxx
RTE
MOVE.W   <ea>,SR
ANDI.W   #word,SR
ORI.W    #word,SR
EORI.W   #word,SR
MOVE.L   USP,An
MOVE.L   An,USP
```

The RESET instruction asserts the reset output from the processor chip, causing all external devices to revert to a standard state. It will usually be one of the first few instructions executed when an operating system or monitor starts up, and will not be executed again in normal running. This instruction has no direct connection with the reset exception, but should be used in the code that the exception jumps to, in order to ensure that all peripherals are in a known state.

The STOP instruction puts the processor into stopped state (which should not be confused with the halted state set after an unrecoverable error). It stops executing instructions until the next interrupt or reset exception occurs. The operand of STOP is a 16-bit immediate value, which is placed in the status register. This allows STOP to set the processor priority level before it stops the machine.

This instruction is intended for use when the computer system based around the 68000 has peripheral devices capable of direct memory access (DMA). This means that they can read from or write to the memory directly, without having to interrupt the 68000 itself. It is usual for a disc device to be connected using DMA, so that it can transfer large chunks of data quickly between memory and disc, and interrupt the running program only when the transfer has finished. A DMA device will often want to use the memory at the same time as the processor, so there is some circuitry which arbitrates and makes one wait for the other. If the program in the 68000 initiates some DMA transfer of data, and then has nothing useful to do until the transfer finishes, then it could just go into a loop until the interrupt comes. However, this makes unnecessary accesses to the memory (to fetch the instructions of the loop) and so may slow down the DMA transfer. It is better to use STOP to stop the 68000 completely when it has nothing to do.

The operand of STOP must have a 1 in the bit corresponding to the supervisor state flag of the status register, otherwise a privilege violation will occur even if STOP is executed in supervisor state. (This is the only way a privilege violation can happen in supervisor state.) Thus, a typical example of this instruction is

```
    STOP    #$2000
```

which sets the interrupt mask to zero, permitting any level of interrupt.

The MOVE to/from USP instructions do not need to be privileged. However, they are intended for use only by programs running in supervisor state, as the user stack pointer is already accessible (as SP) in user state. They are made privileged because any attempt to use them in user state is likely to be due to a programming error which should be brought to the user's attention.

Whenever a privilege violation trap is taken, the saved program counter points at the offending instruction.

Tracing

It is possible to request the 68000 to cause an internal exception after the execution of every instruction. This is the trace exception, and occurs when the trace bit in the status register is on. The saved program counter refers to the instruction after the one saved.

The principal use of the trace exception is as a debugging aid. It allows the program under test to be run one instruction at a time, with control returning to a debugging program after every instruction. This can be a powerful tool for isolating the point at which the error occurs in a faulty program. The monitor in the next chapter provides a tracing facility by using this exception.

The trace exception also greatly simplifies the handling of breakpoints. We saw above how a TRAP instruction can be used to replace the first word of a breakpointed instruction. When the trap is taken, control passes into the debugger, and we can inspect registers, store locations and so on. However, a difficulty arises when we want to continue execution of the program after hitting the breakpoint. We would like the breakpoint to remain in force in case the program reaches that point again, but, in order to continue, we must execute the instruction that has had a TRAP planted on it. What we need to do is to restore that instruction, execute it, and then put back the TRAP in its place before proceeding. Having a trace exception allows this to be done: the instruction is executed with the trace flag on, so control passes back to the debugger, which can put back the breakpoint TRAP and then allow execution to continue normally with the trace flag off.

Bus errors and address errors

A bus error is an attempt to read from or write to an address which does not belong to any device outside the processor. Bus errors are usually caused by trying to use a memory address which does not correspond to any physical memory. The only way that this error can be detected is by observing that no response is forthcoming when the address is used. The detection is performed by logic outside the processor, so that the designer can decide what is a suitable time to wait for a response. If this time limit were built-in to the processor, then it might be impossible to use it with some slow devices.

An address error is an attempt to read or write a word or long word of data at an odd memory address. It is very similar to a bus error, but is detected by the processor itself, and uses a different exception vector.

It can be difficult to determine exactly what caused a bus or address error. It may be due to an invalid operand address within the current instruction, but it might have happened while trying to pre-fetch the next instruction. Also, whereas most exceptions are either processed between instructions, or forced by an instruction, these errors can be noticed at an arbitrary point in the processing of the instruction. This means that the value of the program counter saved will point somewhere near the offending instruction, but may not point exactly at it.

To make it possible to decide what was wrong, the processor saves more information on the stack than for other exceptions. Seven words of stack are used altogether, with the following layout

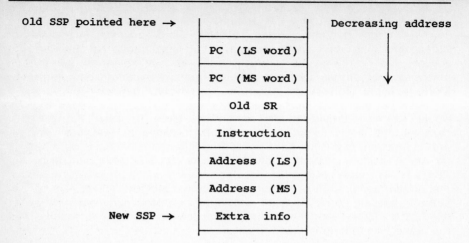

Old SSP pointed here → | Decreasing address

PC (LS word)
PC (MS word)
Old SR
Instruction
Address (LS)
Address (MS)
Extra info

New SSP → Extra info

The instruction field holds the first word of the instruction which was being processed at the time of the bus or address error. This allows the exception handling routine to search back from the saved program counter to find the start of the instruction in store. The address field holds the address to which access was being attempted. The last word contains some extra information about the aborted bus cycle. Its format is as shown

Bit 15   4 3 2 1 0

| | W | N | F |

The W bit is 1 if the access was a write, and 0 otherwise. The N bit is 1 if the 68000 was not processing either an instruction or an exception caused directly by an instruction when the error occurred. This could mean that it was in the stopped state (after a STOP instruction), or already processing one of the other kinds of exception. The F field gives the 3-bit number which was being presented on the function code output lines from the chip. These are the lines which classify the access as supervisor or user, and program or data, and which can be used to divide up the memory into four address spaces.

If the exception vector for bus errors, address errors, or reset contains an invalid or odd address, then a bus or address error will occur while the exception is being processed. This is known as a 'double bus fault', and is treated as an unrecoverable failure. The processor gives up and halts itself, so as not to corrupt any of the evidence in memory. The only way to restart it is to give it an external Reset signal.

In general the 68000 is not capable of continuing with an instruction which caused a bus error, as it might have been in the middle of its internal execution. The 68010 and 68020 save much more information on the stack, thus allowing the instruction which caused the bus error to be resumed.

Multiple exceptions

It is sometimes the case that several exceptions happen very close together, and it may be important to know the order in which they will be handled. The various exceptions can be placed in three distinct groups according to exactly when the exception is processed.

Group 0:   Reset, bus error, address error
The execution of the current instruction is aborted.

Group 1:   Trace, interrupts, privilege violations, illegal instructions
The current instruction is allowed to complete, and the exception is taken just before the next instruction starts. Privilege and illegal instruction traps occur just before the offending instruction would have been executed.

Group 2:   TRAP, TRAPV, CHK, division by zero
The exception occurs as part of the normal instruction execution.

There is a priority order of exceptions, which determines exactly what happens when several are outstanding at once. The highest priority one is processed first, and then the others, in decreasing priority order. The order is (highest first)

Reset
Bus error
Address error
Trace
Interrupts
Illegal instruction, privilege violation (cannot happen together)
TRAP, TRAPV, CHK, division by zero (cannot happen together)

When the trace flag is set, there is no trace exception when the current instruction is aborted by a reset, bus error, or address error. If an interrupt is pending after a traced instruction, then the trace trap is taken before the interrupt. However, if the current instruction forces an exception, then that is processed before the trace exception.

A store size finding routine

We can use the bus error exception in a routine which determines the amount of memory available on our computer. A routine like this is usually executed by an operating system when it starts running so that the same operating system can be loaded into machines with different amounts of store, and will always make use of all that is available.

The routine works by stepping up the memory, trying to access each byte in turn. Eventually it will try to touch one which does not exist, causing a bus error exception to occur. Before the main loop is entered, the bus error exception vector is set up to point to an instruction in this routine (at label SSF_BERR). We do not actually need any of the information stored on a bus error, so can just reset the stack pointer to its original value.

It is possible that the memory address decoding hardware is arranged in such a way that the bus error logic will not detect attempts to access memory just past the highest location that actually exists. To guard against this, the routine checks each byte to see if it does indeed function as memory, by storing a bit pattern and then seeing if it is still there. The bit pattern chosen contains both 1s and 0s, as non-existent memory is likely to appear as either all 1s or all 0s. The original contents of each byte are saved in a register and restored after the test, so that memory remains unaltered. We must be careful not to test the memory in which our program resides, as we would at some point alter a byte in the next instruction to be executed, with unfortunate results! This routine starts the test just after its last byte.

```
* Set A0 to the size of available memory in bytes.
*
* The test starts from the end of this routine, and assumes
* that there is one contiguous block of memory.

MEMPAT  EQU     $AA             Pattern used for memory test
I_BERR  EQU     $8              Address of bus error exception vector

* Plug bus error trap vector to call code here

        MOVE.L  I_BERR,D0       Use D0 to save old trap address
        MOVEA.L SP,A6           Save old stack pointer
        LEA     SSF_BERR,A0     Address for trap
        MOVE.L  A0,I_BERR       Plug trap vector

* Start the search from the byte after the end of this routine

        LEA     SSF_END,A0      Get address for start of search

* Main loop of store size finder

SSFLOOP MOVE.B  (A0),D1         Save byte (may cause bus error)
        MOVE.B  #MEMPAT,(A0)    Load pattern
        CMPI.B  #MEMPAT,(A0)    See if there is memory there
        BNE.S   SSF_FOUND       Have hit top of store
*
        MOVE.B  D1,(A0)+        Restore old contents & go up one byte
        BRA.S   SSFLOOP         Only exit by branch or bus error

* Bus error trap comes here

SSF_BERR MOVEA.L A6,SP          Reset system stack pointer

* Memory size found: in A0 in bytes

SSF_FOUND MOVE.L D0,I_BERR      Restore bus error trap address
SSF_END
```

Chapter 8

A complete example: a monitor

In this chapter we present a complete example. This is a small monitor which will supply a limited range of facilities for running and debugging assembler programs. Such a monitor would normally reside in read only memory, and a real monitor would probably have a great deal more commands than those described here. However the example demonstrates the way in which the 68000 interrupt and trap vectors are used and the use of the supervisor and user modes.

The monitor is intended to reside in any location in memory, and some care has been taken to ensure that the code is all position independent. The monitor itelf runs in supervisor mode, while a user program may be executed only in user mode.

Commands are provided to examine and alter the user's register set, to set and clear breakpoints, to examine and alter memory locations, and to start a user program either normally or in trace mode.

The current value of the user's registers may be printed by using the R command; this will print the value of all the registers. Alternatively the value of a specific address register or data register may be printed by using the A or D command. Similarly the program counter and status register may be selectively printed by the P and S commands.

The contents of any register may be updated by following one of the A, D, P or S commands with a value in hexadecimal. A memory location may be opened by means of the M command, once this has been done the byte at the address specified after the M will be printed.

A further set of commands are provided once a memory location has been opened in this way. A memory location is initially opened as a byte value, but the word (two bytes) or long word (four bytes) starting at that address may be specified by typing W or L, while S restores the size to a single byte. Odd numbered bytes may not be opened as word or long.

Monitor commands	
Ar Ar n	Print value of user address register r Update user address register r to value n
B Bi Bi n	Print current breakpoints Clear breakpoint i Set breakpoint i at location n
C	Continue after a breakpoint
Dr Dr n	Print value of user data register r Update user data register r to value n
G G n	Start user program at current user program counter Start user program at address n
M n	Open memory location n and handle memory commands
P P n	Print value of user program counter Update user program counter to value n
R	Print the value of all user registers
S S n	Print value of user status register Update user status register to value n
T T n	Trace user program from user program counter Trace user program starting at address n

Once a memory location has been opened a new value may be entered in hexadecimal. This will replace four, two or one bytes depending on the currently selected size. The uparrow symbol (^) will open the previous location in the currently selected size, while 'return' opens the next location. The equals symbol (=) may be used to print out the current location again, which is useful if the memory address is actually a memory mapped I/O location. The memory subcommand level is terminated by a fullstop (.), which returns to the normal monitor.

A user program would normally have to be entered into memory by means of the M command, specifying the program in hexadecimal. A more complete monitor would have facilities for loading a program from another computer.

Memory commands	
return	Move to next memory location
^	Move to previous memory location
=	Print current location again
.	Exit memory update command
n	Update current location to value n
L	Print as long value (4 bytes)
S	Print as byte value (1 byte)
W	Print as word value (2 bytes)

Once a program has been entered into memory it may be executed by the G command. This causes the computer to enter user mode and to jump to the location specified in the user program counter. A new value for the program counter may be specified after the G command if required.

In order to debug a program, the T command can also be used to start execution. In this case one instruction is executed and control returns to the monitor again. The register values are printed out, and another monitor command may be issued. However if just a 'return' is typed at this stage, the next instruction is executed. This makes it simple to trace through a program step by step.

The monitor also allows breakpoints to be set in a user program. The B command by itself prints all current breakpoints; Bn deletes breakpoint n and Bn followed by a hexadecimal number sets breakpoint n at the specified address. Once a breakpoint is executed control returns to the monitor. The T command can be used to trace a few instructions, or the C command will continue past the breakpoint.

All exceptions and traps are handled. TRAP #15 is used to indicate that a user program has terminated, while TRAP #14 is used to cause breakpoints. The TRACE vector is used while tracing user programs. All other traps or exceptions cause a suitable message to be written and the user program to be terminated with the contents of the registers saved. After a breakpoint or trace the contents of the registers are printed. In addition, after a trace exception has occurred, the response 'return' will cause another instruction to be traced.

The only interrupt location used is the level 2 auto-vector location; it is assumed that an ACIA will interrupt here. The ACIA location is held as a long value in the program so that this could be patched to alter the actual location of the ACIA in the memory map. Similarly the two areas of RAM used by the monitor for the stack and for other data locations are defined by two other long values within the program.

Constant definition and exception handlers

The first requirement is to define various constants used and to specify the layout of RAM locations. This first section defines various ASCII constants, bits within the status register and some default values. It also specifies the binary opcode for TRAP 14 which is used as a breakpoint.

```
SPACE    EQU    ' '            ASCII space character
CR       EQU    $0D            ASCII carriage return
LF       EQU    $0A            ASCII line feed
BS       EQU    $08            ASCII backspace
DEL      EQU    $7F            ASCII delete
TBIT     EQU    7              Trace bit in saved status register
SBIT     EQU    5              Supervisor bit in it
INTSOFF  EQU    $2700          Interrupts off
INTSON   EQU    $2000          Interrupts on
ISTK     EQU    $4000          Initial stack pointer
INTVECS  EQU    0              Location of fixed vectors
BRKTRP   EQU    $4E4E          TRAP 14 instruction
DEFSP    EQU    $2000          Default USP
```

This next section defines the structure of the RAM area used. We do not use fixed locations as workspace, but instead always use an offset from an address register (usually A6). We need three pointers into a line buffer and the buffer itself in order to handle input characters typed. We also allocate space for the user's registers and for the breakpoint locations. We also provide names for offsets within the user's register save area.

```
BUFWR    EQU    0              Write pointer
BUFRD    EQU    BUFWR+4        Read pointer
BUFLS    EQU    BUFRD+4        Line start pointer
BUFBEG   EQU    BUFLS+4        Buffer area
BUFEND   EQU    BUFBEG+79      End of buffer
RDUMPD   EQU    BUFEND+1       Space for 8 data registers
RDUMPA   EQU    RDUMPD+32      Space for 7 address registers
RDUMPSP  EQU    RDUMPA+28      Space for USP
RDUMPSR  EQU    RDUMPSP+4      Space for user status register
RDUMPPC  EQU    RDUMPSR+2      Space for user program counter
BRKP     EQU    RDUMPPC+4      10 breakpoints, 6 bytes each
BFLG     EQU    BRKP+60        Space for breakpoint flag
RAMEND   EQU    BFLG+2         End of RAM area
*
D_A0     EQU    RDUMPA-RDUMPD  Offset of register A0
D_A7     EQU    RDUMPSP-RDUMPD Offset of register A7
D_SR     EQU    RDUMPSR-RDUMPD Offset of status register
D_PC     EQU    RDUMPPC-RDUMPD Offset of user program counter
RDSIZE   EQU    (RAMEND-RDUMPD)/4 Size of save area in long words
```

Having completed all our definitions we will now proceed to allocate some constant areas. This first area defines the exception, interrupt and trap locations. They are placed at the start of the program in case the code is loaded to start at location zero; in this case they will be in the correct place assuming that the hardware of the machine does not provide different memory areas for program and data. The initialisation section of the monitor also copies these locations into memory starting at zero in case the program is loaded somewhere else. The first two long locations define the initial values for the stack and program counter which are picked up when the 68000 is reset. In order for this to work the whole monitor must be loaded at location zero or else the first eight bytes must be mapped by hardware into the first address within the monitor. In the latter case the start address will have to be relocated in a suitable fashion.

```
TS
I_RESET DC.L     ISTK          RESET stack pointer
        DC.L     START         RESET program counter
        DC.L     B_EXCPT-TS    Bus error
        DC.L     A_EXCPT-TS    Address error
        DC.L     I_EXCPT-TS    Illegal instruction
        DC.L     D_EXCPT-TS    Divide by zero
        DC.L     C_EXCPT-TS    CHK exception
        DC.L     O_EXCPT-TS    TRAPV exception
        DC.L     P_EXCPT-TS    Privilege exception
I_TRACE DC.L     T_EXCPT-TS    Trace exception
        DC.L     X_EXCPT-TS    L1010 emulation (illegal instruction)
        DC.L     Y_EXCPT-TS    L1111 emulation (illegal instruction)
        DS.L     12            Unassigned as yet
        DC.L     S_EXCPT-TS    Spurious interrupt
*
* Autovectored interrupts
*
        DC.L     INT-TS        Interrupt level 1
        DC.L     CINT-TS       Interrupt level 2 (console)
        DC.L     INT-TS        Interrupt level 3
        DC.L     INT-TS        Interrupt level 4
        DC.L     INT-TS        Interrupt level 5
I_INT6  DC.L     INT-TS        Interrupt level 6
I_INT7  DC.L     INT7-TS       Interrupt level 7
*
* Trap vectors
*
        DC.L     TRP-TS        Unexpected TRAP
        DC.L     TRP-TS
        DC.L     TRP-TS
        DC.L     TRP-TS
        DC.L     TRP-TS
        DC.L     TRP-TS
        DC.L     TRP-TS
        DC.L     TRP-TS
        DC.L     TRP-TS
        DC.L     TRP-TS
        DC.L     TRP-TS
        DC.L     TRP-TS
        DC.L     TRP-TS
        DC.L     TRP-TS
        DC.L     TRP14-TS      Breakpoints
```

```
I_BRK     DC.L     TRP15-TS      User requests
*
INTSIZE EQU      (I_BRK-I_RESET)/4 Size of fixed vectors
```

Finally we specify the location of the ACIA and of the RAM area used. This is placed into program space so that these locations can be patched without assembling the entire program all over again.

```
ACIA     DC.L     $83FF01      Address of ACIA
RAMBASE DC.L     $1000        RAM base pointer
```

Input and output

We can now start the code proper. The first few subroutines are intended to be called by any user program, and hence do not expect any registers to have particular values. In the later subroutines which handle the various monitor commands it is assumed that the last character typed is in register D0 and that register A6 points to the base of the RAM area.

The first routine to be defined is the interrupt routine. This will be called whenever a character has been typed at the keyboard, as the address of the start of the routine has been placed in the autovector for interrupt level 2. It must take the character and attempt to place it into a circular buffer. If this is not possible because the buffer is full the character will simply be ignored. If the character is 'rubout' then the last character typed will be removed unless there are no more characters left on the current line.

Normally the character typed will be reflected at the terminal. If 'rubout' is typed then the reflection will be backspace, space, backspace in order to remove the character from the terminal screen. If 'return' is typed then the reflection will be 'return' followed by 'linefeed'.

It is of course vital to save any registers used in an interrupt routine as it may be called at any time. Notice also the use of RTE which replaces the saved status register before returning to whatever code was being executed at the time.

The circular buffer is maintained by three pointers. BUFWR is used as the current write position, and points at the last character entered in the buffer. In the normal case this pointer is incremented via the subroutine INCPTR which takes account of the circular buffer and the new character placed in the buffer at that point. The pointer BUFRD is used to indicate how far the read routine has got in removing characters from the buffer. If the BUFWR reaches BUFRD then there is no more room in the buffer. The read routine will only extract characters from the buffer once an entire line has been typed, thus allowing characters to be deleted. The pointer BUFLS is set to point to the start of the current line both to enable the read routine to check this and so that rubouts are ignored if the entire line has already been deleted. When a rubout is typed the BUFWR pointer is cyclically decremented.

Character reflection is handled by the routine WRCH which writes the character held in D0 to the output part of the ACIA and hence to the terminal. Although an ACIA can be configured to interrupt when the output request has finished this is not used in this example; interrupts are only generated when an input character arrives. As the monitor is only intended to run one program at a time there is nothing that could usefully be done while we wait for the ACIA to complete a transmission. Using reception interrupts means that characters may be typed ahead at any time.

```
*
* Console interrupt routine
*
CINT    MOVEM.L  D0/A1/A2/A6,-(SP) Save registers
        MOVEA.L  ACIA,A1        Get address of ACIA
        MOVE.B   2(A1),D0       Get character and cancel interrupt
        ANDI.B   #$7F,D0        Strip parity bit
        MOVEA.L  RAMBASE,A6     Establish pointer to base area
        MOVEA.L  BUFWR(A6),A2 Get write pointer
        CMP.B    #DEL,D0        Is this delete?
        BNE.S    CINT2          No.. handle normal character
        CMPA.L   BUFLS(A6),A2 Start of line?
        BEQ.S    CINT4          Yes .. nothing to do
        LEA.L    BUFBEG(A6),A1 Get pointer to buffer start
        CMPA.L   A1,A2          If equal then cyclic decrement
        BNE.S    CINT1          No .. normal decrement
        LEA.L    BUFEND(A6),A2 Yes .. set to buffer end
CINT1   SUBQ.L   #1,A2          Decrement pointer
        MOVEA.L  ACIA,A1        Restore ACIA pointer into A1
        MOVE.B   #BS,D0         Get backspace into D0
        BSR.S    WRCH           And send it
        MOVE.B   #SPACE,D0      Next a space
        BSR.S    WRCH           And send that
        MOVE.B   #BS,D0         Finally another backspace
        BRA.S    CINT3          Send it after updating write pointer
CINT2   BSR.S    INCPTR         Update pointer handling circular list
        CMPA.L   BUFRD(A6),A2 Check equal to read pointer
        BEQ.S    CINT4          Equal, so no room in buffer
        MOVE.B   D0,(A2)        Store character
CINT3   MOVE.L   A2,BUFWR(A6) Store write pointer back again
        BSR.S    WRCH1          Write character in D0 to ACIA in A1
        CMPI.B   #CR,D0         Is this a return?
        BNE.S    CINT4          No .. nothing else to do
        MOVE.L   A2,BUFLS(A6) Update line start pointer
        MOVE.B   #LF,D0         Place line feed code in D0
        BSR.S    WRCH1          And display it
CINT4   MOVEM.L  (SP)+,D0/A1/A2/A6 Restore registers
        RTE                     And return from interrupt
```

This little subroutine assumes that A2 contains a pointer into the circular buffer, and that A6 points to the base of the RAM area. It increments A2 and resets it to the start of the buffer if it has reached the end.

```
INCPTR  MOVE.L   Al,-(SP)        Save register
        ADDQ.L   #1,A2           Increment pointer
        LEA.L    BUFEND(A6),Al   Get pointer to end of area
        CMPA.L   Al,A2           Check if equal
        BNE.S    INCl            No, so ok
        LEA.L    BUFBEG(A6),A2   Reset pointer to start of buffer
INC1    MOVE.L   (SP)+,Al        Restore register
        RTS
```

The next few routines are concerned with output. The first routine is WRCH, which transmits the character held in D0 to the output section of the ACIA. It uses a subsidiary routine WRCH1 which assumes that A1 points to the ACIA.

```
WRCH    MOVE.L   Al,-(SP)        Save register
        MOVEA.L  ACIA,Al         Extract ACIA address
        BSR.S    WRCH1           Transmit character
        MOVE.L   (SP)+,Al        Restore Al
        RTS
```

The routine WRCH1 is called by WRCH and WRITES after setting up A1 to point to the ACIA control register. The ACIA data register appears in memory two bytes higher. It simply waits for the ACIA to become ready and then transmits the character held in D0.

```
WRCH1   BTST     #1,(Al)         Check if ACIA is ready for output
        BEQ.S    WRCH1           No, wait until it is
        MOVE.B   D0,2(Al)        Transmit character
        RTS
```

The next few routines are just generally useful subroutines to do with output. BLANK writes a space to the output while NEWLINE writes carriage return followed by linefeed to the output.

```
BLANK   MOVE.L   D0,-(SP)        Save D0
        MOVEQ    #SPACE,D0       Space code
        BSR.S    WRCH            Write it
        BRA.S    NEWL2           Jump to shared code
*
* Write out a CR, LF to the output
*
NEWLINE MOVE.L   D0,-(SP)        Save D0
        MOVEQ    #CR,D0          Print carriage return
        BSR.S    WRCH
        MOVEQ    #LF,D0          Print line feed
        BSR.S    WRCH
NEWL2   MOVE.L   (SP)+,D0        Restore D0
        RTS
```

This is a variation on a routine we have already seen. WRITES is called with A0 pointing to some characters terminated by a zero byte. The characters are all written to the output. It calls WRCH1 rather than WRCH as it sets up the pointer to the ACIA once and for all at the start of printing the string.

Finally it branches to NEWLINE to print a newline at the end of the string. This demontrates a common trick. If the last action of a subroutine is to call another routine and then to execute an RTS instruction it is simpler to branch directly to that subroutine. The return address for WRITES will still be on the stack, so that when NEWLINE finally executes its own RTS the jump is made back to the caller of WRITES.

```
WRITES   MOVEM.L DO/AO-A1,-(SP) Save registers
         MOVEA.L ACIA,A1        Extract ACIA address
WRITES1  MOVE.B  (AO)+,DO       Extract character from string
         BEQ.S   WRITES2        Zero - end of string
         BSR.S   WRCH1          Write out character using ACIA in A1
         BRA.S   WRITES1
WRITES2  MOVEM.L (SP)+,DO/AO-A1 Restore registers
         BRA.S   NEWLINE        Print newline and return
```

The final set of output routines are used to print hexadecimal numbers. WRHEX4 prints four hexadecimal bytes, WRHEX2 prints two and WRHEX1 prints a single byte. Finally WRHEX0 prints four bits, or a 'nibble'. Any of these routines can be called individually although they all end up calling WRHEX0 the required number of times. Note that register values are not corrupted as they are swapped around and then replaced.

WRHEX4 swaps register halves to print out the top two bytes via a call of WRHEX2, and then drops into the code of WRHEX2 to print the bottom two bytes.

```
WRHEX4   SWAP    DO             Swap high and low halves
         BSR.S   WRHEX2         Write high 2 bytes
         SWAP    DO             Swap high and low halves again
* Drop through to WRHEX2
```

WRHEX2 performs a similar trick. It rotates the low order word to print the high order byte of the pair via a call of WRHEX1, and then rotates it back again to restore the register. It then drops through to the code of WRHEX1 to print the low order byte.

```
WRHEX2   ROR.W   #8,DO          Shift top byte down to low order
         BSR.S   WRHEX1         Write single byte
         ROL.W   #8,DO          Shift bottom byte back again
* .. and drop into WRHEX1 for this byte
```

WRHEX1 is very similar to WRHEX2. In this case the top four bits are rotated down so that they may be printed by WRHEX0, then rotated back and the bottom four bits printed.

```
WRHEX1   ROR.B   #4,DO          Shift down top nibble
         BSR.S   WRHEX0         Write it out
         ROL.B   #4,DO          Put back bottom nibble
*    .. and drop into WRHEX0
```

Finally WRHEX0 actually writes out a single hexadecimal digit held in DO. It takes care not to corrupt DO, and calls WRCH to handle the output.

```
WRHEX0   MOVE.L   D0,-(SP)        Save register
         ANDI.B   #$0F,D0         Mask to bottom 4 bits
         ADDI.B   #'0',D0         Add character zero
         CMPI.B   #'9',D0         Test to see if greater than char 9
         BLS.S    WRHEX01         Just write it
         ADDI.B   #'A'-'9'-1,D0   Convert to character
WRHEX01  BSR.S    WRCH            Write out hex character
         MOVE.L   (SP)+,D0        Restore register
         RTS                      And return
```

The last part of this section concerns input routines. The opposite of WRCH is RDCH which returns a character from the terminal in register D0. It is convenient to clear the high order three bytes of D0 and to return the character in the low order byte.

We must remember the circular line buffer maintained by the interrupt routine, and the fact that two pointers BUFRD and BUFLS point to the last character read out of the buffer and the start of the current line respectively. We compare the read pointer BUFRD with the start of line pointer BUFLS, and if these are the same then we loop waiting until they are not. This will happen, of course, when the interrupt routine has accepted a 'return' from the keyboard which indicates that the user has completed his line of input. If characters have been typed ahead then there is no need to wait and we can extract them at once. We also call the same routine INCPTR to step a pointer through the circular buffer.

```
RDCH     MOVEM.L  A2/A6,-(SP)     Save registers
         MOVEA.L  RAMBASE,A6      Pointer to data area
         MOVEA.L  BUFRD(A6),A2    Extract buffer read pointer
RDCH1    CMPA.L   BUFLS(A6),A2    Equal to line start?
         BEQ.S    RDCH1           Wait until it is not
         BSR      INCPTR          Increment buffer read pointer
         MOVEQ    #0,D0           Clear all of D0
         MOVE.B   (A2),D0         Extract character
         MOVE.L   A2,BUFRD(A6)    Update buffer read pointer
         MOVEM.L  (SP)+,A6/A2     Restore registers used
         RTS
```

This routine reads a hexadecimal number from the keyboard. Two entry points are provided. READHEX reads the next character from the input, while READH assumes that the next character has already been read and is sitting in register D0. The result is returned in D1, and D0 is set to the last character read by the routine. If an invalid character is found the Z bit is unset, if all goes well the Z bit is set. This can be tested later with BNE to jump to some sort of error handler.

```
READHEX  BSR.S    RDCH            Get character
READH    CMPI.B   #SPACE,D0       Check if space
         BEQ.S    READHEX         Discard leading spaces
         CLR.L    D1              Clear result register
RDH1     CMPI.B   #'0',D0         Check if below character 0
```

```
          BCS.S    RDH4           Error exit with Z unset
          CMPI.B   #'9',D0        Check if above character 9
          BHI.S    RDH2           Possibly A .. F
          SUBI.B   #'0',D0        Subtract character 0
          BRA.S    RDH3           And assemble in D1
RDH2      BSR      LOCASE         Convert to lower case
          CMPI.B   #'a',D0        Check if below character a
          BCS.S    RDH4           Error exit with Z clear
          CMPI.B   #'f',D0        Check if above character f
          BHI.S    RDH4           Error exit with Z clear
          SUBI.B   #'a'-10,D0     Convert to correct value
RDH3      ASL.L    #4,D1          Multiply current sum by 16
          ADD.L    D0,D1          Add in this term
          BSR.S    RDCH           Get next character
          CMPI.B   #CR,D0         See if equal to CR
          BEQ.S    RDH4           Yes.. exit with Z set
          CMPI.B   #SPACE,D0      See if equal to space
          BNE.S    RDH1           No .. go back and handle it
RDH4      RTS                     Exit with Z set if all ok
```

Branch table handling

Within the monitor we will want to take a command letter from the input and to determine some action on the basis of the letter typed. We shall use the routine SEARCH to perform this. It expects a character in D0 and a pointer to a branch table in register A0.

The branch table indicates the required action for each valid character, and a default action if the character is not valid. Each entry in the table consists of four bytes. The first byte is a flag which is set to zero if there are more entries in the table and set non-zero if there are no more entries. In this case the entry in the table is to be taken as representing the default action required.

The second byte in each entry holds the character with which the specified action is associated. It is ignored when the flag byte is set.

The final two bytes are used to indicate the action to be performed. For each action there is an associated subroutine, and the address of this subroutine is indicated in the two byte slot. In order to maintain position independent code the entry in the table represents the offset of the subroutine from the base of the table.

We use a branch table for two reasons. Firstly the same code can be used to decode different sets of commands which are valid in different circumstances. Here we shall use SEARCH to decode normal commands and memory change commands. Secondly it makes it easy to add new commands, simply by providing a new entry in the table and a subroutine to do the job.

The routine SEARCH is passed a character in register D0 which is converted into lower case, by the routine LOCASE. Each entry in the table is checked to see if it contains this character; if a match is found in the table the associated routine is called. If the non-zero flag byte at the end of the table is encountered the routine specified is always called.

No registers are corrupted by this subroutine. In order to achieve this we use the stack as workspace. Firstly the original value of D0 is restored by reading it from the penultimate stack frame slot; this slot is then updated with the address of the subroutine which is to be called. Register A0 is then restored and the stack pointer lowered so that the stack contains the required entry point, followed by the return address to whatever called SEARCH. The final RTS instruction then picks this value off the stack and hence jumps to the required subroutine, which will return to the caller of SEARCH if it executes an RTS.

```
SEARCH  MOVE.L  D0,-(SP)      Save register D0
        MOVE.L  A0,-(SP)      and register A0
        BSR.S   LOCASE        Convert to lower case
SRCH1   TST.B   (A0)+         Check if end and skip byte
        BNE.S   SRCH2         Non zero - end of table
        CMP.B   (A0)+,D0      Compare character and skip byte
        BEQ.S   SRCH3         Found it!
        ADDQ.L  #2,A0         Skip routine offset
        BRA.S   SRCH1         And try again
SRCH2   ADDQ.L  #1,A0         Skip unused character byte
SRCH3   MOVEA.W (A0),A0       Offset of routine from table base
        ADDA.L  (SP),A0       Add in saved table base
        MOVE.L  4(SP),D0      Restore register D0
        MOVE.L  A0,4(SP)      And replace with routine address
        MOVE.L  (SP)+,A0      Restore register A0
        RTS                   Pickup routine address and jump to it
```

The following small routine converts the character in register D0 to lower case if required. Once we have established that the character requires conversion we add a value which represents the difference between lower and upper case letters.

```
LOCASE  CMPI.B  #'A',D0       Check if alphabetic character
        BCS.S   LOC1          No need to convert unless it is
        CMPI.B  #'Z',D0       Check again
        BHI.S   LOC1          Still no need
        ADDI.B  #'a'-'A',D0   Convert character to lower case
LOC1    RTS                   And return
```

Initialisation and command handling

The next section of code is the initialisation section of the monitor, and the label START is the entry point for the entire program. We have placed this address in the reset vector so that this program will be called when the machine is turned on or reset.

The first action is to turn interrupts off, as the interrupt handlers are not yet defined and so any interrupts would be embarassing. We then issue the RESET command to simulate an external reset in case this entry point was simply jumped to. We then reset the ACIA which is not affected by the 68000 reset.

```
START    MOVE.W   #INTSOFF,SR    Interrupts off, supervisor mode
         RESET                   Issue RESET command
         MOVEA.L  ACIA,A3        Point to ACIA
         MOVE.B   #$03,(A3)      Reset ACIA
```

The next step is to copy the interrupt handlers into their defined slots in RAM. If the program is loaded at zero then they will be in the correct place anyway, but no harm will be done copying them back on top of themselves unless the program is held in ROM and the hardware is set up to indicate a bus error if ROM is written to. In most hardware configurations this would not be the case.

We also wish to maintain position independence, and so the value stored in the table is not the actual address but the offset of the required address from the base of the program. Again this will be correct if the program is loaded starting at location zero, and if not then we simply add the address of the base of the program to each of the offsets to obtain the correct addresses.

```
         LEA.L    INTVECS,A1     Point to interrupt vector area
         LEA.L    I_RESET,A2     Point to defined handlers
         MOVE.L   A2,D2          Maintain base pointer
         MOVE.W   #INTSIZE,D0    Number of slots
STO      MOVE.L   (A2)+,D1       Extract handler location
         ADD.L    D2,D1          Add table base
         MOVE.L   D1,(A1)+       Install in low RAM
         DBRA     D0,STO         loop until complete
```

The next step is to set up the system stack pointer which is obtained from the value stored in the reset vector. Again, this is only required if the entry point has been jumped to rather then entered because of an external reset. Once this has been done we can safely turn interrupts on again.

```
         MOVE.L   I_RESET,SP     Initial system stack
         MOVE.W   #INTSON,SR     Interrupts on again
```

We can now initialise the ACIA and set up the correct initial values for the pointers into the circular buffer used by the ACIA interrupt handler. We also establish A6 as our pointer to the base of the RAM that we are using. This value is expected to remain in A6 while the monitor is running.

```
         MOVEA.L  RAMBASE,A6     Establish RAM address register
         LEA.L    BUFBEG(A6),A1  Point to buffer start
         MOVE.L   A1,BUFWR(A6)   Initial buffer write pointer
         MOVE.L   A1,BUFRD(A6)   Initial buffer read pointer
         MOVE.L   A1,BUFLS(A6)   Initial buffer line start pointer
         MOVE.B   #$89,(A3)      Magic value. Rx interrupts on.
```

The next stage is to clear the breakpoint and user register store to zero. We pick up one less than the number of slots as our counter because DBRA stops when the counter is −1. We also set up the initial value for the user stack pointer.

```
        LEA.L    RDUMPD(A6),A1 Point to data save areas
        MOVE.W   #RDSIZE-1,D0 Size of area to clear
CL      CLR.L    (A1)+         Clear data area
        DBRA     D0,CL         Branch until done
        MOVE.L   #DEFSP,RDUMPSP(A6) Set initial USP
```

We are now in a position to write out the header message. We call WRITES to do this, having first loaded A0 with a pointer to the message.

```
        LEA.L    MESS1,A0      Point to header message
        BSR      WRITES        Write message
```

This is the main execution loop, which is very simple. First we write out the prompt, calling WRCH. We then load A0 with a pointer to the table which contains the entry points for the subroutines which handle each command. The subroutine SEARCH is then called which will eventually call the correct routine. If that routine returns we branch back for another command. If the command caused an error or entered a user program we will jump back to label ST1 directly from the exception handling section.

```
ST1     MOVE.B   #'#',D0       Write prompt
        BSR      WRCH
ST2     BSR      RDCH          Get character into D0
        LEA.L    COMTAB,A0     Point to command search table
        BSR      SEARCH        Execute required function
        BRA.S    ST1           And issue prompt again
```

Simple command routines

The rest of the monitor consists of a number of subroutines which are called via the command search table. In all cases these routines are entered with register D0 containing the character which initiated the action, and they may corrupt any register except A6, which is assumed to hold a pointer to the base of the RAM work area. The routines all return to their caller except for those connected with executing a user program (G and T). In this case the entry back into the monitor will occur when an exception takes place.

The first routine is the default routine and is called if an unknown command is entered. It simply prints a message and drops into a standard routine to skip to the end of the typed input line.

```
COMERR  LEA.L    MESS2,A0      Point to message
        BSR      WRITES        Print it
```

This next subroutine is called when most other command subroutines are about to finish. It simply reads and ignores anything else which may follow the command on the input line. D0 must contain the last character read from the input in case that was a carriage return. This routine is also called as the response to a return typed at the console.

```
SKIPNL  CMPI.B  #CR,DO        Check if DO is CR
        BEQ.S   SKIPNL1       If so then exit
        BSR     RDCH          Otherwise ignore characters
        BRA.S   SKIPNL        Until it is one
SKIPNL1 RTS                   And return
```

The next set of routines are called when an error has been detected. The first is used when a number was expected but not found. Because it calls SKIPNL register DO must contain the last character read from the line.

```
NUMERR  LEA.L   MESS3,AO      Point to message
        BSR     WRITES        Print it
        BRA.S   SKIPNL        And skip line
```

The next is almost the same and is called when an invalid memory change command has been found.

```
MEMERR  LEA.L   MESS4,AO      Point to message
        BSR     WRITES        Print it
        BRA.S   SKIPNL        And skip line
```

Register display and update

The following routines handle the commands which display and alter the contents of the user's registers. The first is REG which is called after the R command has been entered. It simply displays the contents of all the user's registers. There are in fact two entry points. REG is used when the R command has been given, and REGX is used when the registers are to be displayed after a trace or breakpoint exception. The only difference is that the REG entry point skips the rest of the command line, if any.

The first few lines print out the user program counter and status register, using WRHEX4 and WRHEX2 respectively. Note that it is assumed that register A6 refers to the base of the RAM work area.

```
REG     BSR     SKIPNL        Skip rest of line
REGX    MOVEQ   #'P',DO       Register letter into DO
        BSR     WRCH          Write it out
        MOVEQ   #'C',DO       And next letter
        BSR     WRCH          Write that
        BSR     BLANK         And a space
        MOVE.L  RDUMPPC(A6),DO Obtain user PC
        BSR     WRHEX4        Write it out
        BSR     BLANK         Space
        MOVEQ   #'S',DO       Register letter
        BSR     WRCH          Write out
        MOVEQ   #'R',DO       And the next
        BSR     WRCH          Write that
        BSR     BLANK         And a space
        MOVE.W  RDUMPSR(A6),DO Obtain user SR
        BSR     WRHEX2        Write out 2 bytes
```

```
        BSR     NEWLINE      And a newline
```

The next lines print out the data registers and the address registers. Because of the similarity in printing the two different types, REG1 is a subroutine which is called once with the register letter 'D' held in D1 and A3 pointing to the start of the data register save area. When REG1 returns A3 is left pointing to the start of the address registers. The register letter is updated to contain 'A', and REG1 is entered again by dropping into it rather than calling it as a subroutine.

```
        LEA.L   RDUMPD(A6),A3 Point to data registers
        MOVEQ   #'D',D1      Register letter into D1
        BSR.S   REG1         Display register set
        MOVEQ   #'A',D1      Register letter
*  .. and drop through
```

The REG1 section of code prints out the value of the eight user registers saved in the memory location pointed at by A3. It identifies the registers using the letter held in D1. It calls WRHEX0 to write the register number and WRHEX4 to write the value. Subroutines BLANK and NEWLINE are called where required to ensure that we get four registers per line suitably spaced. The address register A3 is incremented through the register save area as the register values are printed, and so is left pointing to just beyond the end of the region when the task has been completed.

```
REG1    MOVEQ   #0,D2        D2 is register number
REG2    MOVE.B  D1,D0        Extract register letter
        BSR     WRCH         Write register letter
        MOVE.B  D2,D0        Register number
        BSR     WRHEX0       Write nibble of that
        BSR     BLANK        Write out space
        ADDQ.B  #1,D2        Update register number
        MOVE.L  (A3)+,D0     Extract register value
        BSR     WRHEX4       Write it out
        CMP.B   #8,D2        All done yet?
        BEQ.S   REG3         All over
        BSR     BLANK        Print another space
        CMP.B   #4,D2        Register 4 next?
        BNE.S   REG2         No, so print once more
        BSR     NEWLINE      Newline before register 4
        BRA.S   REG2         And print next line
REG3    BRA     NEWLINE      Final newline and exit
```

There are four commands provided to alter or inspect the value of a particular user register. The A and D commands are each followed by a register number. If no value is given after the register name the value is printed. Otherwise a hexadecimal value is read and the register in question is set to this new value.

The routines for D and A share common code once register A3 has been set up to point to the start of the data or address register save area.

```
SETD    LEA.L   RDUMPD(A6),A3 Set A3 to data register store
        BRA.S   SETR          Jump to common code
*
* Address register
*
SETA    LEA.L   RDUMPA(A6),A3 Set A3 to address reg store
```

This section of common code first reads the register number following the letter D or A. It calls READHEX and checks the value returned to see if it is valid. If not then a jump to SETRE is made, which is a common error exit for all of the register update commands. If the value is correct it is multiplied by four to provide a byte offset into the data register store.

```
SETR    BSR     READHEX
        BNE.S   SETRE       Register number expected
        TST.L   D1          Check bounds
        BLT.S   SETRE       Error
        CMP.L   #7,D1       Upper bound
        BGT.S   SETRE       Error
        MOVE.W  D1,D3       Save in D3
        ASL.W   #2,D3       Multiply by four
```

The next part of the code is also shared by the P command, which examines or alters the user's program counter. First the last character read from the input is checked to see if it was a return. This is returned from READHEX in register D0. If no value follows the current value is printed out at label SETR2.

If the line did not terminate with a return the value specified is read using the READH entry point to READHEX. This ensures that whatever character is held in D0 is taken into account when reading the hexadecimal value. If an error is detected in this a jump is made to the standard code at NUMERR. Otherwise the value is inserted into the correct slot, which is identified as the offset computed from the register number and the base register A3 which either points to the data or address register save area. Finally the routine returns through SKIPNL which skips any other text on the line.

```
SETR1   CMP.B   #CR,D0      See if any value given
        BEQ.S   SETR2       No, so print value
        BSR     READH       Get value, last character in D0
        BNE     NUMERR      Hex number expected
        MOVE.L  D1,0(A3,D3.W) Insert value in correct slot
        BRA     SKIPNL      Skip rest of line & return
```

The label SETR2 is reached if no new value was specified. In this case the current value is extracted from the correct slot in the register save area and printed out.

```
SETR2   MOVE.L  0(A3,D3.W),D0 Extract register value
        BSR     WRHEX4      Print it out
        BRA     NEWLINE     Finish with NL
```

The subroutine SETP is called when the P command is used to alter or examine the user's program counter. This value can also be updated by specifying a value after the G or T command. It simply loads A3 with a pointer to the program counter save area and sets the offset for the register number to zero. This ensures that when the shared code at label SETR1 is entered the correct location will be referenced. Before it jumps there it reads the next character from the input into D0. This is because D0 will be set to contain the last character read when READHEX has been called in the previous cases.

```
SETP    LEA.L   RDUMPPC(A6),A3 Point to PC store
        CLR.W   D3             Offset zero
        BSR     RDCH           Get next character
        BRA.S   SETR1          Jump to shared code
```

The S command is used to print or change the user's status register. The subroutine involved cannot share the same code as the preceding routines because the status register is only a word sized object. We do not check the value of the status register — if the user wishes to set the trace bit then his code will be traced. We do not allow the supervisor bit to be set when the program is started, but no check is made at this point.

```
SETS    BSR     RDCH           Read next character
        CMP.B   #CR,D0         Check if new value given
        BEQ.S   SETS1          No, print current value
        BSR     READH          Get value, last character in D0
        BNE     NUMERR         Error in value
        MOVE.W  D1,RDUMPSR(A6) Update saved copy of SR
        BRA     SKIPNL         Return
SETS1   MOVE.W  RDUMPSR(A6),D0 Extract current value
        BSR     WRHEX2         Print it out
        BRA     NEWLINE        Print newline & return
```

The final part of the register change section simply prints a message if an invalid register number has been given.

```
SETRE   LEA.L   MESS6,A0       Message
        BSR     WRITES         Print it out
        BRA     SKIPNL         Skip rest of line & return
```

Entering a user program

This section implements the T, G and C commands which are used to enter a user's program. The entry point TGO is used for the T command, and GO for the G command. The TGO entry point simply sets the trace bit in the saved copy of the user's status register. The CONT entry point is used for the C command, which continues executing a user program past a breakpoint.

The first step is to see if an entry point for the user's program has been given. If no value has been given then a jump is made to the label GO1. Otherwise the entry point is read using the READH entry point to READHEX because the current character is already held in D0. If there is no error then the saved copy of the user's program counter is updated with the new value.

```
* Trace mode requested
TGO      BSET    #TBIT,RDUMPSR(A6) Set trace bit in saved SR
* Normal mode requested
GO       BSR     RDCH            Get next character
         CMP.B   #CR,D0          Check for simple case
         BEQ.S   GO1             Start program running
         BSR     READH           Read entry point, D0 last char read
         BNE     NUMERR          Error in number
         MOVE.L  D1,RDUMPPC(A6) Update saved PC
```

Label GO1 starts a user program running. This code can also be entered from the exception handler when a program has been interrupted because of a trace exception, and the next instruction is to be traced.

The first job is to check that the supervisor bit is not set in the copy of the user's status register. If this is so the program will not be run.

```
GO1      BTST    #SBIT,RDUMPSR(A6) Check supervisor bit not set
         BNE.S   GOERR           Error if so
         CLR.B   BFLG(A6)        Clear breakpoint flag
```

The next stage is to insert breakpoints into the user's code. Breakpoints are only inserted when the program is about to be run so that if the user examines his code it appears unchanged. The addresses where breakpoints are to be placed are held in the table BRKP. This contains six bytes per entry. The first four bytes hold the address for the breakpoint or zero if this breakpoint is not used. The last two bytes are used to hold the original code which is replaced by the two byte instruction TRAP #14. We move the breakpoint address into D1 because we wish to detect if it is zero - remember that MOVEA does not alter condition codes. As we wish to also use this value as an address later, we clear A2 to zero. This means that the construction 0(A2,D1.L) effectively allows us to use D1 as an address register.

There is an added complication concerned with actually executing the code which should reside in the memory location where we have placed a breakpoint. Having reached a breakpoint it is very common to trace on for a few instructions. In this case we do not want to insert the breakpoint trap, instead we want to actually execute the instruction. For this reason we also check to see if the breakpoint is about to be placed at the address given by the user's program counter. If so then we do not insert the breakpoint this time. Note that we do in fact take a copy of the instruction so that when all the breakpoints are removed in the exception handler we can insert the correct code back in without making another special case.

In order to continue past breakpoints the special command C must be used. This uses the fact that a breakpoint will not be set at the current program counter address. Firstly it sets the trace bit, then jumps to the label CGO. We will therefore execute the instruction at the breakpoint address, and enter the monitor again due to the trace exception. We set a special flag called BFLG which is set to a non-zero value when we have just given the C command. The exception handler will check this flag, and unless it is zero it will simply restart the program using the standard G routine. This ensures that the breakpoint is replaced in the correct place ready to be executed again if required. We have already set the flag BFLG to zero so that this special processing will not take place if T or G were specified.

```
CGO     MOVEA.L  RDUMPPC(A6),A4 Extract user PC
        LEA.L    BRKP(A6),A1    Point to breakpoint space
        MOVEQ    #9,D0          Counter
        SUBA.L   A2,A2          Zero A2
GO2     MOVE.L   (A1)+,D1       Breakpoint address
        BEQ.S    GO3            Zero address so no breakpoint
        MOVE.W   0(A2,D1.L),(A1) Save original instruction
        CMPA.L   D1,A4          Check if breakpoint at user PC
        BEQ.S    GO3            Do not insert breakpoint if so
        MOVE.W   #BRKTRP,0(A2,D1.L) Replace with breakpoint trap
GO3     ADDQ.L   #2,A1          Increment A1
        DBRA     D0,GO2         Try next breakpoint
```

We are now ready to start the user program running. First we extract the saved copy of the user stack pointer into register A0, and then into the user stack pointer USP. This is required because only address registers can be moved into USP.

The next step is to extract the user's program counter and status register and save them on the system stack, ready for the subsequent RTE instruction. We then reload all the user's registers from the save area with an enormous MOVEM, and then execute RTE which resets the status register and program counter. Because the status register does not have the supervisor bit set we will end up running the user's program in user mode. The only way in which the program will return control to the monitor is if an exception occurs, and we have reserved TRAP 15 as the way in which a user program signifies that it has ended.

```
        MOVE.L   RDUMPSP(A6),A0 Extract user stack pointer
        MOVE.L   A0,USP         And set it up
        MOVE.L   RDUMPPC(A6),-(SP) Stack user PC
        MOVE.W   RDUMPSR(A6),-(SP) Stack user SR
        MOVEM.L  RDUMPD(A6),D0-D7/A0-A6 Setup user's registers
        RTE                     Hold tight
```

The C command is used to continue after a breakpoint. The standard test for supervisor bit set is made, the trace bit is turned on and the code branches to label CGO in order to start the user program. As the user program counter will be equal to the breakpoint address the particular breakpoint will not be inserted this time. We also set the flag BFLG to non-zero by using the Scc instruction with the condition TRUE. This will be used in the exception handler to distinguish between a proper trace exception and the trace exception generated after executing the code at which a breakpoint has been placed. In the latter case we will simply replace the breakpoints in the code and continue execution. This ensures that breakpoints appear to the user to be installed all the time.

```
CONT    BSR     SKIPNL          Ignore any other input
        BTST    #SBIT,RDUMPSR(A6) Check not supervisor bit
        BNE.S   GOERR           Error if so
        BSET    #TBIT,RDUMPSR(A6) Set trace bit
        ST      BFLG(A6)        Set marker flag to $FF
        BRA.S   CGO             Enter user program
```

Finally GOERR is branched to if the supervisor bit is set in the saved status register. A suitable error message is printed and further commands requested.

```
GOERR   LEA.L   MESS7,A0        Load ptr to message
        BSR     WRITES          Write it out
        BRA     SKIPNL          Skip line & return
```

Memory examine and update routines

The next set of routines are used to inspect and alter memory. Typing the letter M causes this code to be entered, whereupon the location specified is 'opened' and the value stored there printed out. Subsequent memory change commands are then read which can alter the value in the open location, open another location or return to normal command mode.

Memory locations can be opened as a byte, word or long object. Initially a location is opened as a byte. Register D2 is used to hold the size of the object. Thus if the location is to be opened as a byte D2 will contain 1, if as a word 2, and 4 if it is opened as long. We will keep the current memory location in register A3. The first part of the subroutine takes the location and prints the address of it out.

```
MEM     BSR     READHEX         Read location
        BNE     NUMERR          Error in number
        MOVEA.L D1,A3           Move address into A3
        MOVEQ   #1,D2           Set up as byte value initially
MEM1    MOVE.L  A3,D0           Move location into D0
        BSR     WRHEX4          And write it out
        BSR     BLANK           Write a space
```

The next step is to look at the size qualifier held D2 and to print a byte, word or long value. This entails extracting a suitable sized value and printing it using WRHEX1, WRHEX2 or WRHEX4.

```
        CMP.B   #2,D2           Check size required
        BLT.S   MEMB            < 2 .. byte
        BEQ.S   MEMW            = 2 .. word
        MOVE.L  (A3),D0         Extract long data
        BSR     WRHEX4          Write out information
        BRA.S   MEMQ
MEMW    MOVE.W  (A3),D0         Extract word data
```

```
        BSR     WRHEX2          And write out
        BRA.S   MEMQ
MEMB    MOVE.B  (A3),DO         Extract byte
        BSR     WRHEX1          And write out
MEMQ    MOVE.B  #'?',DO         Question mark
        BSR     WRCH            Write that out
```

The next step is to attempt to read a new value. If an error occurs then rather than simply print an error message we go on to see if a valid memory change command was given – in this case D0 will contain the last character read.

```
        BSR     READHEX         Attempt to read new value
        BNE.S   MEM2            If not a number try other command
        BSR     SKIPNL          Skip rest of line
```

In this case a valid number was given, and we must update the memory location. Having done this we do not want to read the same memory location again, as this sometimes causes problems when attempting to place values into memory locations which are in fact registers within I/O chips such as an ACIA. We have a subroutine called NMEM which moves us on to the next memory location, and this must be called. Rather than BSR to it and then branch to MEM1 in three different cases we place the address of MEM1 onto the stack with a PEA instruction. We can then branch to the routine NMEM, which will return to MEM1 when it executes the RTS at the end.

```
        PEA.L   MEM1            Push MEM1 so we will return to it
        CMP.B   #2,D2           Check size again
        BLT.S   MEMBW           Byte
        BEQ.S   MEMWW           Word
        MOVE.L  D1,(A3)         Update long value
        BRA.S   NMEM            Display next value, return to MEM1
MEMWW   MOVE.W  D1,(A3)         Update word value
        BRA.S   NMEM            Display next value, return to MEM1
MEMBW   MOVE.B  D1,(A3)         Update byte value
        BRA.S   NMEM            And display next and return to MEM1
```

In this case an invalid number was read, and the offending character is in D0. We will use the same routine SEARCH to identify the correct action to take, passing it in this case the table MEMTAB. This is of the same form as COMTAB which was used in the main execution loop, but contains address offsets and letters for memory change commands. When any of these return we will still be in the memory change environment. As a special case we see if the exit command (.) has been given and terminate the M command if this is so. We also clear the rest of the input line via a call to SKIPNL after any of the memory commands have finished.

```
MEM2    CMPI.B  #'.',DO         Check for end command
        BEQ.S   MEM3            Exit if so
        LEA.L   MEMTAB,A0       Get memory change response table
        BSR     SEARCH          Call suitable routine
        BSR     SKIPNL          Skip rest of line
```

```
        BRA.S   MEM1            Display again
MEM3    BRA     SKIPNL          Skip rest of line and return
```

The following routines are called via the table MEMTAB and implement the various memory commands. The first simply moves to the next memory location, and is called if a return is typed. It is also called after updating a location. The address size is held in D2, and the current location is in A3.

```
NMEM    ADDA.L  D2,A3           Onto next location
        RTS
```

This is very similar, and moves to the previous location.

```
PMEM    SUBA.L  D2,A3           Back to previous location
        RTS
```

The following routines change the size of the memory accessed. For byte sized values this simply means altering the size held in D2.

```
SETB    MOVEQ   #1,D2           Update D2
        RTS
```

If the location is to be opened as a word or long value, the current address must be even. The subroutine CHKEVEN is called to make this check. The subroutine will only return if the check succeeded. Otherwise it jumps back to the routine which called SETW or SETL.

```
* Set to word value.
SETW    BSR.S   CHKEVEN         Check even, error if not
        MOVEQ   #2,D2           Update D2
        RTS
* Set to long value.
SETL    BSR.S   CHKEVEN         Check if even
        MOVEQ   #4,D2           Update D2
        RTS
```

This routine is used to check if A3 contains an even address. If the check fails the normal return address is ignored and the routine returns to the caller of the routine which called it. This will always be MEM in this case.

```
CHKEVEN MOVE.L  A3,D0           Place A3 in D0
        BTST    #0,D0           Check bottom bit
        BEQ.S   CHK1            Zero so value is even
        LEA.L   MESS5,A0        Point to message
        BSR     WRITES          Print it
        LEA.L   4(SP),SP        Ignore this return address
CHK1    RTS                     Return or error return to MEM
```

Breakpoints

The next routines handle the setting, clearing and listing of breakpoints. We have already noted in the GO routine that a table of breakpoints is maintained. For each breakpoint six bytes are used to hold the address of the breakpoint and the code word which the breakpoint replaces when it is inserted.

In this section we are only concerned with the manipulation of the breakpoint addresses. The B command all by itself simply lists the current breakpoints. Unused breakpoints have an address set to zero, so this is checked and if the breakpoint is set the breakpoint . number and the address is printed out.

```
BRK       LEA      BRKP(A6),A1   Point to breakpoint table
          BSR      RDCH          Read next character
          CMP.B    #CR,D0        Check for simple B command
          BNE.S    BRK1          No, more complex
* Display current breakpoints
          MOVEQ    #0,D1         Counter
BRK0      TST.L    (A1)          Check if set
          BEQ.S    BRK01         No, not set
          MOVE.B   D1,D0         Breakpoint number into D0
          BSR      WRHEX0        Print breakpoint number
          BSR      BLANK         Print space
          MOVE.L   (A1),D0       Extract breakpoint location
          BSR      WRHEX4        Print address
          BSR      NEWLINE       Print newline
BRK01     ADDQ.L   #6,A1         Increment pointer
          ADDQ.B   #1,D1         Increment offset
          CMP.B    #9,D1         Check if done
          BLE.S    BRK0          Loop until done
          RTS                    Return
```

In this case a breakpoint number is expected after the B command. Register D0 will contain the character following this as we have called RDCH earlier, so we use the READH entry point to READHEX to obtain the breakpoint number.

```
BRK1      BSR      READH         Read hex number, char in D0
          BNE.S    BRKE          Error in that
          TST.L    D1            Check within bounds
          BLT.S    BRKE          Too small
          CMP.L    #9,D1         Check other bound
          BGT.S    BRKE          Too big
```

Having satisfied ourselves that the breakpoint number is correct we must work out the correct offset. As there are six bytes per entry we shall have to use the MULS instruction to obtain it. Fortunately there are only ten breakpoints allowed so the limit on the size of the arguments to MULS does not affect us. We then check to see if any value was given after the breakpoint number. If not then we clear the breakpoint, otherwise we set a new one.

```
        MULS    #6,D1           Offset in table
        ADDA.L  D1,A1           Point to slot
        CMP.B   #CR,DO          Any position given?
        BNE.S   BRK2
```

In this case we wish to clear the breakpoint which is pointed at by A1.

```
        CLR.L   (A1)            Clear breakpoint
        RTS                     And return
```

At this stage we must read the value specified and update the breakpoint table.

```
BRK2    BSR     READH           Get position of breakpoint
        BNE     NUMERR          Error in that
        MOVE.L  D1,(A1)         Place address in slot
        BRA     SKIPNL          Skip rest and return
```

The only work left now is to print a message if the breakpoint number was invalid.

```
BRKE    LEA.L   MESS8,AO        Point to message
        BSR     WRITES          Write message
        BRA     SKIPNL          Skip line & return
```

Exception handling

This section of code is concerned with the handling of any exception, interrupt or trap that may occur. The standard action is to print a suitable message after saving the user's registers if required.

The following labels define addresses which have been patched into the correct exception vectors by the initialisation code. At each label a short branch to subroutine instruction takes us to the code to handle the two different types of exception which may occur. A BSR is used so that the return address saved on the stack can be used as an index to determine which interrupt occurred.

```
* Exceptions
B_EXCPT BSR.S   EXCP1           Bus error
A_EXCPT BSR.S   EXCP1           Address error
I_EXCPT BSR.S   EXCP2           Illegal instruction
D_EXCPT BSR.S   EXCP2           Divide by zero
C_EXCPT BSR.S   EXCP2           CHK
O_EXCPT BSR.S   EXCP2           TRAPV
P_EXCPT BSR.S   EXCP2           Privilege
T_EXCPT BSR.S   EXCP2           Trace
X_EXCPT BSR.S   EXCP2           L1010
Y_EXCPT BSR.S   EXCP2           L1111
S_EXCPT BSR.S   EXCP2           Spurious interrupt
* Interrupts
INT     BSR.S   EXCP2           Unexpected interrupt
```

```
INT7    BSR.S   EXCP2           Level 7 interrupt
* Traps
TRP     BSR.S   EXCP2           Unexpected TRAP
TRP14   BSR.S   EXCP2           Breakpoint
TRP15   BSR.S   EXCP2           End of user program
```

In this case we must handle the more complicated case of an address or bus error. Because of the instruction pre-fetch of the 68000 the program counter will be smaller than the saved value on the stack might lead us to believe. There are a number of extra words of information saved on the stack, including the instruction register. We can step the program counter back until the instruction at the program counter matches that stored in the instruction register.

We must be very careful to save all of the user's registers. The layout of the stack is as follows, with the address of the entry point to the monitor saved most recently by the BSR earlier.

```
        ┌─────────────┐
        │  Program    │         Decreasing
        │  Counter    │          Address
        ├─────────────┤
        │ Status Reg  │
        ├─────────────┤
        │  Ins Reg    │              │
        ├─────────────┤              │
        │  Access     │              │
        │  Address    │              ▼
        ├─────────────┤
        │  Fn Code    │
        ├─────────────┤
        │  Entry      │
        │  Address    │
SSP →   └─────────────┘
```

```
EXCP1   MOVEM.L DO/AO,-(SP)     Save some registers
        MOVE.L  22(SP),AO       Program counter
        MOVE.W  18(SP),DO       Instruction register
        CMP.W   -(AO),DO        Decrement PC and compare
        BEQ.S   EXCP10          Equal so ok
        CMP.W   -(AO),DO        Decrement again
        BEQ.S   EXCP10          Ok
        CMP.W   -(AO),DO        Decrement again
        BEQ.S   EXCP10          Ok
        CMP.W   -(AO),DO        Decrement again
        BEQ.S   EXCP10          Ok
        SUBQ.L  #2,AO           No so must be this one
EXCP10  MOVE.L  AO,22(SP)       Restore corrected PC
        MOVEM.L (SP)+,DO/AO     Restore saved registers
        MOVE.L  (SP),8(SP)      Overwrite with return address
        ADDQ.L  #8,SP           Modify SP and drop through ...
```

This represents a simpler type of exception. The system stack now looks as follows.

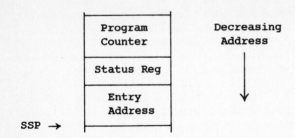

```
        Program          Decreasing
        Counter          Address

        Status Reg

        Entry
        Address

SSP →
```

```
EXCP2   BTST     #SBIT,4(SP)  Test supervisor bit of saved SR
        BNE.S    EXCP3        If set then not user program running
        MOVE.L   A0,-(SP)     Save A0 temporarily
        MOVEA.L  RAMBASE,A0   Point to RAM area
        LEA.L    RDUMPD(A0),A0 Get a pointer to register save area
        MOVEM.L  D0-D7/A0-A6,(A0) Save all the user's registers
        MOVE.L   (SP)+,D_A0(A0) Fix saved value of A0
        MOVE.L   (SP)+,A1     Extract return address caused by BSR
        MOVE.W   (SP)+,D_SR(A0) Update user's SR
        BCLR     #TBIT,D_SR(A0) Ensure trace bit turned off
        MOVE.L   (SP)+,D_PC(A0) Update user's PC
        MOVE.L   USP,A2       Extract USP
        MOVE.L   A2,D_A7(A0)  And place that in A7 slot
```

We have now managed to save all of the user's registers and we must proceed to replace any breakpoints inserted in the code. The original value of the code is held in the last two bytes of each six byte area. Even if the breakpoint has not been inserted because the user's program counter was equal to the breakpoint address a copy of the original instruction will still be held in the breakpoint table.

```
        MOVEA.L  RAMBASE,A6   Re-establish RAM pointer
        LEA.L    BRKP(A6),A3  Point to breakpoint save space
        MOVEQ    #9,D0        Counter
BRKL    MOVE.L   (A3)+,A4     Location of breakpoint
        MOVE.W   (A3)+,D1     Original code
        CMPA.L   #0,A4        Was breakpoint set?
        BEQ.S    BRKL1        No..
        MOVE.W   D1,(A4)      Replace original code
BRKL1   DBRA     D0,BRKL      Loop as required
        BRA.S    EXCP4        Now write message
```

In this case an error (hopefully bus error during M command) occurred while running the monitor. Do not alter user's registers, but give the message as usual.

```
EXCP3   MOVE.L   (SP)+,A1     Extract return address stacked by BSR
```

We now have saved all the user's registers, and A1 contains the address of the next instruction after the one we jumped to via the interrupt vector locations. We must correct this to point to the actual instruction.

We must also reset the system stack to the original value given it when we entered the monitor. After we have done this it is safe to turn interrupts on again, as even if we have a large number of unexpected interrupts we will have reset our stack back to base again before attempting to handle another one.

```
EXCP4    SUBQ.L   #2,A1        Pointer to code we actually entered
         MOVE.L   I_RESET,SP   Reset system stack
         MOVE.W   #INTSON,SR   Interrupts on again
```

We now want to look for two special cases. These are trace exception and breakpoint.

```
         LEA.L    T_EXCPT,A0   Trace exception
         CMPA.L   A0,A1        Was it one?
         BEQ.S    EXCP5        Yes, handle it
         LEA.L    TRP14,A0     Breakpoint trap?
         CMPA.L   A0,A1        Was it this?
         BEQ.S    EXCP6        Handle it
```

At this point it was some other type of exception. We call the subroutine WRABO which writes a message based on the value of A1. This is still pointing at the entry point specific to the abort, and is used to select the correct message. Once this has been done we can branch to the start of the command loop to look for any more commands.

```
         BSR.S    WRABO        Write suitable message
         BRA      ST1          And handle any more commands
```

We get here if a trace exception has occurred. There are two possible reasons for a trace exception. The first is that it was generated by the C command. This sets the trace bit so that once we have executed the instruction normally overwritten by the TRAP #14 used for breakpoints we can replace the breakpoint. If this was the case the flag BFLG will be non-zero, and we simply enter the user's program once again. The breakpoint will then be installed ready for another time.

```
EXCP5    TST.B    BFLG(A6)     Test to see if C was last command
         BNE      GO1          Continue execution if so
```

This handles a normal trace exception. First we write a suitable message using WRABO agin. We then call the entry point REGX of REG to display the registers.

Because it is very common to require one trace after another, we will patch the normal command handling so that the response 'return' is the same as typing T. Any other command will be handled as normal. To do this we make A0 point to the command table, and then use PEA to place the entry point of the main command loop onto the stack.

We write a small letter 't' as a prompt to show that the monitor is in a special mode, and then read the response of the user. If this is not a simple 'return' we branch to the standard SEARCH subroutine to handle it. Because we have placed the address of ST1 onto the stack, when the subroutine called by SEARCH finally returns it will return to ST1 rather than back here.

If the character read in is indeed a return, we set the trace bit and continue execution of the user program by jumping to GO1.

```
        BSR.S   WRABO           Write trace message
        BSR     REGX            Print registers
        LEA.L   COMTAB,A0       Point to command table
        PEA.L   ST1             Push return address of command loop
        MOVE.B  #'t',DO         New prompt character
        BSR     WRCH            Write it out
        BSR     RDCH            Get next character
        CMP.B   #CR,DO          Return?
        BNE     SEARCH          No, do standard search for command
        BSET    #TBIT,RDUMPSR(A6) Set the trace bit in saved SR
        BRA     GO1             And continue execution
```

At this point we must handle a breakpoint. The user will have set a breakpoint at some address which we have patched to contain the TRAP #14 instruction. This always works as TRAP instructions are only one word long, which is the same as the shortest possible instruction. This TRAP #14 will have caused us to arrive here. We have not yet executed the instruction which normally resides at the breakpoint address. Therefore the first thing to do is to decrement the program counter by two bytes.

We then write a suitable message and call REGX to display the state of the registers. We can then branch to ST1 to read any subsequent commands. When the user asks for the program to be continued we will not insert the breakpoint which caused this trap because the breakpoint address will be equal to the program counter. Control will return to the monitor immediately after the instruction has been executed if C or T commands were used, and we will then be in a position to replace the TRAP 14 instruction when the user program is next restarted.

```
EXCP6   SUBQ.L  #2,RDUMPPC(A6)  Back up user PC
        BSR.S   WRABO           Write breakpoint message
        BSR     REGX            Display registers
        BRA     ST1             And ask for another command
```

The final subroutine in our monitor uses the value stored in register A1 to write a suitable message corresponding to the exception which has just happened.

We have already adjusted A1 so that it is the address of the label at which the exception handler was entered. We load the address of the first possible label into A0 and subtract the two. As each BSR.S instruction takes up a word, the result will be a word offset corresponding to the exception type. This is then used as an index into the table ABOTAB. Each entry in ABOTAB is the offset from the base of the table of a string describing the error. We add the base of the table to the string offset to give us the string address which is then written out using WRITES.

```
WRABO   LEA.L   B_EXCPT,A0    Base of table
        SUBA.L  A0,A1         Now a word offset from zero
        LEA.L   ABOTAB,A2     Pointer to abort table base
        MOVE.L  A1,D0         Offset into D0
        MOVE.W  0(A2,D0.L),A0 Offset of string from table base
        ADDA.L  A2,A0         Add table base to point to string
        BRA     WRITES        Write it out and return
```

Messages and tables

All that remains now is to define the messages and tables used in the monitor. Firstly the error messages generated as a result of the user typing something we don't like, and our initial message.

```
MESS1   DC.B    'MC68000 monitor V1.2',0
MESS2   DC.B    'Unknown command',0
MESS3   DC.B    'Hexadecimal number expected',0
MESS4   DC.B    'Invalid memory command',0
MESS5   DC.B    'Current address not even',0
MESS6   DC.B    'Invalid register number',0
MESS7   DC.B    'Supervisor bit set',0
MESS8   DC.B    'Invalid breakpoint number',0
```

Next we have the messages relating to exceptions, unexpected interrupts and traps.

```
AB1     DC.B    'Bus error',0
AB2     DC.B    'Address error',0
AB3     DC.B    'Illegal instruction',0
AB4     DC.B    'Division by zero',0
AB5     DC.B    'CHK exception',0
AB6     DC.B    'TRAPV exception',0
AB7     DC.B    'Privilege violation',0
AB8     DC.B    'Trace...',0
AB9     DC.B    'Illegal instruction (1010)',0
AB10    DC.B    'Illegal instruction (1111)',0
AB11    DC.B    'Spurious interrupt',0
AB12    DC.B    'Unexpected interrupt',0
AB13    DC.B    'Level 7 interrupt',0
AB14    DC.B    'TRAP exception',0
AB15    DC.B    'Breakpoint',0
AB16    DC.B    'End of user program',0
```

The addresses of the preceding messages are stored in the following table. They are stored as offsets from the table base to preserve position independence. The ordering in the table corresponds to the ordering of the labels used to enter the exception handler.

```
ABOTAB  DC.W    (AB1-ABOTAB )
        DC.W    (AB2-ABOTAB )
        DC.W    (AB3-ABOTAB )
        DC.W    (AB4-ABOTAB )
        DC.W    (AB5-ABOTAB )
        DC.W    (AB6-ABOTAB )
        DC.W    (AB7-ABOTAB )
        DC.W    (AB8-ABOTAB )
        DC.W    (AB9-ABOTAB )
        DC.W    (AB10-ABOTAB )
        DC.W    (AB11-ABOTAB )
        DC.W    (AB12-ABOTAB )
        DC.W    (AB13-ABOTAB )
        DC.W    (AB14-ABOTAB )
        DC.W    (AB15-ABOTAB )
        DC.W    (AB16-ABOTAB )
```

The following two tables are in the correct form for the SEARCH subroutine. This means that the first byte of each four byte entry is zero except for the last entry in the table. The second byte contains the lower case version of a character, while the next two bytes refer to a subroutine to be called if the character read matches the character in the entry. The subroutine is specified as an offset from the base of the table. The last entry in each table has the first byte set to a non-zero value, and the specified routine is always called.

This first table is used to handle to normal commands.

```
COMTAB  DC.W    CR              Just a return
        DC.W    (SKIPNL-COMTAB )
        DC.W    'm'             Memory change
        DC.W    (MEM-COMTAB )
        DC.W    'r'             Register dump
        DC.W    (REG-COMTAB )
        DC.W    'd'             Alter data register
        DC.W    (SETD-COMTAB )
        DC.W    'a'             Alter address register
        DC.W    (SETA-COMTAB )
        DC.W    'p'             Alter PC
        DC.W    (SETP-COMTAB )
        DC.W    's'             Alter SR
        DC.W    (SETS-COMTAB )
        DC.W    'g'             Enter user program
        DC.W    (GO-COMTAB )
        DC.W    't'             Trace user program
        DC.W    (TGO-COMTAB )
        DC.W    'b'             Breakpoint
        DC.W    (BRK-COMTAB )
        DC.W    'c'             Continue after breakpoint
        DC.W    (CONT-COMTAB )
        DC.W    $FF00           Marker flag for end
        DC.W    (COMERR-COMTAB )
```

Finally we have the table used to decode memory subcommands issued after an M command.

```
MEMTAB  DC.W    CR              Move to next location
        DC.W    (NMEM-MEMTAB)
        DC.W    '^'             Up arrow
        DC.W    (PMEM-MEMTAB) Previous memory location
        DC.W    '='             Equals
        DC.W    (SKIPNL-MEMTAB) Stay at same location
        DC.W    's'             Set to byte size
        DC.W    (SETB-MEMTAB)
        DC.W    'w'             Set to word size
        DC.W    (SETW-MEMTAB)
        DC.W    'l'             Set to long size
        DC.W    (SETL-MEMTAB)
        DC.W    $FF00           Marker flag for end
        DC.W    (MEMERR-MEMTAB) Memory change error
        END
```

Name	Description	Size	N Z V C X	Page
ABCD	Add decimal Modes: ABCD Dn,Dn ABCD -(An),-(An)	B	U P U C C	78

ADD
ADDA
ADDI
ADDQ
ADDX
	Add binary
	
	Modes: ADD <ea>,Dn
	        ADD Dn,<maea>
	        ADDA <ea>,An
	        ADDI #<imm>,<daea>
	        ADDQ #<imm>,<aea>
	        ADDX Dn,Dn
	        ADDX -(An),-(An)
		BWL
		WL
		BWL
		BWL
		BWL
			C C C C C
			- - - - -
			C C C C C
			A A A A A
			C P C C C
				67
				67
				68
				68
				68

AND ANDI ANDI to CCR ANDI to SR	Logical AND (privileged) Modes: AND <dea>,Dn AND Dn,<maea> ANDI #<imm>,<daea> ANDI #<imm>,CCR ANDI #<imm>,SR	BWL BWL B W	C C O O - C C O O - P P P P P P P P P P	84 84 84 84
ASL ASR	Arithmetic shift left Arithmetic shift right Modes: ASL Dn,Dn ASL #<imm>,Dn ASL <maea>	BWL BWL	C C C C C C C C C C	86 86
Bcc BRA BSR	Branch on condition Branch unconditionally Branch to subroutine Modes: Bcc <label>	BW BW BW	- - - - - - - - - - - - - - -	39 39 54
BCHG BCLR BSET BTST	Bit test and change Bit test and clear Bit test and set Bit test Modes: BCHG Dn,<daea> BCHG #<imm>,<daea> BTST Dn,<dea> BTST #<imm>,<dea>	B L B L B L B L	- C - - - - C - - - - C - - - - C - - -	87 87 87 87
CHK	Check and possibly TRAP Modes: CHK <dea>,Dn	W	U U U U -	101

Name	Description	Size	N Z V C X	Page
CLR	Set to zero Modes: CLR <daea>,Dn	BWL	0 1 0 0 -	41

CMP
CMPA
CMPI
CMPM
	Compare
	
	Modes: CMP <ea>,Dn
	        CMPA <ea>,An
	        CMPI #<imm>,<daea>
	        CMPM (An)+,(An)+
		BWL
		WL
		BWL
		BWL
			C C C C -
			C C C C -
			C C C C -
			C C C C -
				37
				38
				38
				38

DBcc DBRA	Decrement test and branch Decrement and branch Modes: DBcc Dn,<label>	W W	- - - - - - - - - -	44 44
DIVS DIVU	Division (signed) Division (unsigned) Modes: DIVS <dea>,Dn	W W	C C C 0 - C C C 0 -	75 75
EOR EORI EORI to CCR EORI to SR	Logical Exclusive OR (privileged) Modes: EOR Dn,<daea> EORI #<imm>,<daea> EORI #<imm>,CCR EORI #<imm>,SR	BWL BWL B W	C C 0 0 - C C 0 0 - P P P P P P P P P P	84 84 84 84
EXG	Exchange registers Modes: EXG Rn,Rn	L	- - - - -	70
EXT	Sign extend Modes: EXT Dn	WL	C C 0 0 -	70
JMP JSR	Jump Jump to subroutine Modes: JMP <cea>	- -	- - - - - - - - - -	58 59
LEA	Load effective address Modes: LEA <cea>,An	L	- - - - -	60
LINK	Subroutine link Modes: LINK An,#<imm>	-	- - - - -	63
LSL LSR	Logical shift left Logical shift right Modes: LSL Dn,Dn LSL #<imm>,Dn LSL <maea>	BWL BWL	C C 0 C C C C 0 C C	85 85

Name	Description	Size	N Z V C X	Page
MOVE	Move data	BWL	C C 0 0 −	33
MOVEA		WL	− − − − −	35
MOVEM	Move multiple	WL	− − − − −	51
MOVEP	Move to peripheral	WL	− − − − −	48
MOVEQ		L	C C 0 0 −	42
MOVE to CCR		W	C C C C C	98
MOVE to SR	(privileged)	W	C C C C C	98
MOVE from SR		W	− − − − −	98
MOVE USP	(privileged)	L	− − − − −	96

	Modes: MOVE <ea>,<daea>
	          MOVEA <ea>,An
	          MOVEM <rl>,−(An)
	          MOVEM <rl>,<caea>
	          MOVEM (An)+,<rl>
	          MOVEM <cea>,<rl>
	          MOVEP Dn,d(An)
	          MOVEP d(An),Dn
	          MOVEQ #<imm>,Dn
	          MOVE <dea>,CCR
	          MOVE <dea>,SR
	          MOVE SR,<daea>
	          MOVE USP,An
	          MOVE An,USP			

MULS	Multiply (signed)	W	C C 0 0 −	70
MULU	Multiply (unsigned)	W	C C 0 0 −	70
	Modes: MULS <dea>,Dn			
NBCD	Negate decimal	B	U P U C C	78
	Modes: NBCD <daea>			
NEG	Negate binary	BWL	C C C C C	69
NEGX		BWL	C P C C C	69
	Modes: NEG <daea>			
NOP	No operation	−	− − − − −	16
	Modes: NOP			
NOT	Logical complement	BWL	C C 0 0 −	83
	Modes: NOT <daea>			
OR	Logical OR	BWL	C C 0 0 −	83
ORI		BWL	C C 0 0 −	84
ORI to CCR		B	P P P P P	84
ORI to SR	(privileged)	W	P P P P P	84
	Modes: OR <dea>,Dn OR Dn,<maea> ORI #<imm>,<daea> ORI #<imm>,CCR ORI #<imm>,SR			

Name	Description	Size	N Z V C X	Page
PEA	Push effective address Modes: PEA <cea>	L	− − − − −	61
RESET	Reset (privileged) Modes: RESET	−	− − − − −	101
ROL ROXL ROR ROXR	Rotate left Rotate right Modes: ROL Dn,Dn ROL #<imm>,Dn ROL <maea>	BWL BWL BWL BWL	C C 0 C − C C 0 C C C C 0 C − C C 0 C C	86 86 86 86
RTE RTR RTS	Return from exception Return and restore CCR Return from subroutine Modes: RTE	− − −	C C C C C C C C C C − − − − −	98 98 55
SBCD	Subtract decimal Modes: SBCD Dn,Dn SBCD −(An),−(An)	B	U P U C C	78
Scc	Set from condition Modes: Scc <daea>	B	− − − − −	43
STOP	Stop execution and wait Modes: STOP #<imm>	−	C C C C C	102

SUB
SUBA
SUBI
SUBQ
SUBX
	Subtract binary
	
	Modes: SUB <ea>,Dn
	SUB Dn,<maea>
	SUBA <ea>,An
	SUBI #<imm>,<daea>
	SUBQ #<imm>,<aea>
	SUBX Dn,Dn
	SUBX −(An),−(An)
		BWL
		WL
		BWL
		BWL
		BWL
			C C C C C
			− − − − −
			C C C C C
			C C C C C
			C P C C C
				69
				69
				69
				69
				69

SWAP	Swap register halves Modes: SWAP Dn	W	C C 0 0 −	70
TAS	Test bit and set Modes: TAS <daea>	B	C C 0 0 −	88

Name	Description	Size	N Z V C X	Page
TRAP TRAPV	Cause TRAP exception TRAP if overflow Modes: TRAP #<imm> TRAPV	– –	– – – – – – – – – –	
TST	Compare with zero Modes: TST <daea>	BWL	C C 0 0 –	
UNLK	Subroutine unlink Modes: UNLK An	–	– – – – –	

Conditional tests

The following may be specified as the conditional test in Bcc, DBcc and Scc instructions. In addition, T and F may be used to indicate true and false respectively in DBcc and Scc instructions. Some assemblers allow the additional syntax DBRA for DBF and the tests HS and LO for CC and CS.

In the table, C indicates that the C status bit must be set, and C' means that the bit must be unset for the condition to be true. Conditions may be connected by & (meaning both must be true) or | (meaning either may be true).

Name	Condition	Test
CC	Carry clear	C'
CS	Carry set	C
EQ	Equal	Z
NE	Not equal	Z'
PL	Plus	N'
MI	Minus	N
VC	Overflow clear	V'
VS	Overflow set	V
HI	High (logical GT)	C' & Z'
LS	Low or same (logical LE)	C	Z
HS	High or same (logical GE)	C'
LO	Low (logical LT)	C
GT	Greater than	(N & V & Z')	(N' & V' & Z')
GE	Greater than or equal	(N & V)	(N' & V')
LE	Less than or equal	Z	(N & V')	(N' & V)
LT	Less than	(N & V')	(N' & V)

Index